Greatest Feats

Greatest Feats

ISBN: 1-931933-15-4
Manufactured in the United States of America
First Printing 2002

GREATEST FEATS: SPORT'S MOST UNFORGETTABLE ACCOMPLISHMENTS

Editorial Director: Morin Bishop
Project Editor: Jeff Labrecque
Managing Editor: Theresa M. Deal
Writer/Researchers: Andrew Blais, John Bolster, Kate Brash, Ward Calhoun
Copy Editor: Lee Fjordbotten
Photography Editor: John S. Blackmar
Designers: Barbara Chilenskas, Vincent Mejia, Miki Sakai

GREATEST FEATS: SPORT'S MOST UNFORGETTABLE ACCOMPLISHMENTS
was prepared by
Bishop Books, Inc.
611 Broadway
New York, New York 10012

TIME INC. HOME ENTERTAINMENT
President   Rob Gursha
Vice President, Branded Businesses   David Arfine
Executive Director, Marketing Services   Carol Pittard
Director, Retail & Special Sales   Tom Mifsud
Director of Finance   Tricia Griffin
Marketing Director   Kenneth Maehlum
Product Manager   Dana Pecoraro
Prepress Manager   Emily Rabin
Associate Product Manager   Victoria Alfonso
Associate Product Manager   Ann Gillespie

Special thanks to: Suzanne DeBenedetto, Robert Dente, Gina Di Meglio, Anne-Michelle Gallero,
Peter Harper, Natalie McCrea, Jessica McGrath, Jonathan Polsky, Mary Jane Rigoroso, Steven Sandonato,
Bozena Szwagulinski, Niki Whelan.

We welcome your comments and suggestions about SPORTS ILLUSTRATED Books.
Please write to us at:
SPORTS ILLUSTRATED Books
Attention: Book Editors
PO Box 11016
Des Moines, IA 50336-1016

If you would like to order additional products, please call us at 1-800-327-6388.
(Monday through Friday, 7:00 a.m.–8:00 p.m. or Saturday, 7:00 a.m.–6:00 p.m. Central Time)
Please visit our website: www.TimeBookstore.com

10 9 8 7 6 5 4 3 2 1

CONTENTS

INTRODUCTION

By Jack McCallum

To my knowledge, there is no treatise rating the most splendid performances of a Russian ballet, or the most emotional revivals of an O'Neill play, or the most show-stopping, string-searing gigs of Hendrix. We sports folks, though, have an endless need to classify and categorize, to measure, evaluate and debate endlessly about the relative merits of long jumpers and jump shooters, to gleefully assess why this apple is superior to that orange and defend our positions with grim-faced Rumsfeldian passion.

I happen to think that Wilt Chamberlain's 100-point game in 1962 pales in comparison, as a classic performance, to 17-year-old Pele's scoring two goals in the 1958 World Cup. Wanna make something of it?

Greatest Feats represents the most ambitious venture yet into the sports achievement-appraisal game. Four distinct types of exploits are recognized: Classic Performances (such as Mark Spitz's seven gold medals in Munich), Spectacular Seasons (such as Oscar Robertson's triple-double year in 1961–62), Legendary Streaks (such as Bud Wilkinson's Oklahoma football teams winning 47 straight games from 1953 to '57) and A Lifetime of Excellence (such as Jerry Rice's 195 career touchdowns). Each chapter

Rice is arguably the greatest player in NFL history.

Adversity conditioned Armstrong (left) and Unitas (above) to develop the consistency that fueled two great streaks.

includes several accompanying stories. Wouldn't you like to know, for example, how Joe DiMaggio's legendary 56-game hitting streak was almost stopped? Or the close call Byron Nelson had en route to his winning 11 straight golf tournaments in 1945?

Sports rolls along, for the most part, on the rails of its daily routine. Baseball players are measured over 162 games, not, as Harvey Haddix was, on a single May night when he pitched 12 perfect innings only to lose in the 13th. But it is the classic exploits, those moments of singular magnificence that give sport its texture, its fullness. The majority of us can't recall much of what happened in an otherwise forgettable

November 1970 meeting between the New Orleans Saints and the Detroit Lions, but we remember Saints placekicker Tom Dempsey putting his right foot on the ball and launching it 63 yards for a game-winning field goal.

The wonderful thing about Haddix and Dempsey is that they were not Hall of Famers but, rather, service-able performers who caught lightning in a bottle. Is there any other form of human endeavor that presents such an opportunity? If the Baptist preacher happens, on one magical Sunday, to reach the oratorical heights of Martin Luther King Jr., no one except for the members of his small congregation will know it. But Haddix

Heiden (above) and Woods (right) achieved legendary status by steamrolling the best competition the world had to offer.

and Dempsey live on. At the same time, it's interesting—but hardly surprising—how many of sport's immortals produced classic performances: Michael Jordan can be found here, along with Eric Heiden, Lance Armstrong, Tiger Woods and Secretariat.

True greatness, of course, comes over the long haul, and *Greatest Feats* assesses all kinds of hauls. For all of Johnny Unitas's flat-topped excellence, one single achievement typifies his career as the greatest Baltimore Colt of them all. This book tells you what that is. We know Martina Navratilova was the most dominating women's tennis player of her genera-

tion—maybe of all generations—but what 1984 feat truly proves that? Stay tuned and we'll tell you.

I was on press row in Sydney, Australia, in 2000 when one of sport's greatest achievements—Alexander Karelin's 13-year unbeaten streak in Greco-Roman wrestling—was ended by a then obscure American named Rulon Gardner. As I went off to chase Gardner—the new story—I was struck by how quickly we forgot about Karelin, the more historically significant story. This book won't let you do that. At the same time, it will allow you to compare your judgments with ours. My guess is, you'll want to make something of it.

CLASSIC PERFORMANCES

INTRODUCTION

While some of the finest performances in sports history have been produced by athletes who had otherwise unremarkable careers, more often than not, a single, immortal performance is as indicative of greatness as smoke is of fire.

Sure, there are the unusual cases like Harvey Haddix, a good but not great pitcher who on May 26, 1959, produced arguably the finest single outing in baseball history (*see page 26*). But Haddix and his ilk are the exception. Good athletes will occasionally catch lightning in a bottle, but legendary ones are like Ben Franklin with a kite and a key in a thunderstorm. They make a career out of electrifying outings.

Thus, our "Classic Performances" chapter includes feats achieved by Haddix, Johnny Vander Meer and Tom Dempsey, but its ranks are dominated by the exploits of Jesse Owens, Pelé and Michael Jordan. These are the athletes who provided the performances for the ages, and most of their signature feats are instantly recognizable to the average sports fan, like Nadia Comaneci's perfect 10s at the Montreal Olympics, or Jordan's 63-point game against the Boston Celtics in the 1986 playoffs. That game announced to the basketball world that a special talent had arrived. It moved no less a roundball deity than Larry Bird to say, "I think he's God disguised as Michael Jordan."

Spectators in Mexico City could be excused for thinking a similar supernatural intervention was at work during the long jump competition at the 1968 Olympic Games. That was the site of our highest ranked classic performance, Bob Beamon's astonishing leap of 29' 2".

In ranking each feat, we gave special consideration to its significance in sports history, the likelihood that it will ever be matched and the stage on which it occurred. Beamon shattered the world record—along with notions of what was pos-

The classic performances of Johnson (opposite) in 1996, Grange (left) in 1924 and Comaneci (above) in 1976 made permanent marks in history.

sible at the time—by nearly two feet, and he did it on track and field's grandest stage, the Olympics. The record has since been surpassed, but its significance can hardly be overstated. As physiologist Ernst Jokl said, Beamon's leap was "a mutation performance." It spawned a new word in the sportwriter's lexicon, "Beamonesque," which took its rightful place alongside "Ruthian."

Hard on Beamon's heels in our rankings is a man thoroughly unaccustomed to trailing anyone, sprinter Jesse Owens. Here we honor not his epochal performance at the 1936 Berlin Olympics, but a feat he accomplished a year earlier, when he was a student at Ohio State. At the 1935 Big Ten Championships, Owens set or tied six world records in a 45-minute span.

Pounding the backstretch behind Owens is the mighty Secretariat, whose 31-length victory in the 1973 Belmont remains unmatched in the annals of thoroughbred racing. Secretariat became an instant icon of the 1970s, much like the athlete in our fourth spot, swimmer Mark Spitz, who won seven gold medals and set seven world records in the '72 Games, then appeared on a best-selling poster wearing nothing but his Speedo and his medals. Two places behind Spitz is another Olympic golden boy, speed skater Eric Heiden, who won five gold medals at the Lake Placid Games in 1980.

The following pages are filled with athletes of comparable star power, encompassing legends from the 1930s (Owens and Red Grange), the '50s (Roger Bannister and Ben Hogan), the '70s (Bill Walton and Comaneci) and the '90s (Jordan and Michael Johnson). Together they form a kaleidoscope of sporting images and stories, with one thing in common—the time-tested quality of a classic.

23

LION TAMER

> *Tom Dempsey gave the Big Easy something to celebrate when he kicked a record 63-yard field goal to beat the Detroit Lions in 1970.*

Tom Dempsey wasn't the typical NFL kicker. He was born with a withered right arm and half a right foot, and at 6' 2", 255 pounds as an adult, he was built more like a lineman than a kicker. Wearing a specially-made square shoe, though, he was capable of booming kicks. In his rookie season of 1969, he had nailed a 55-yard field goal for the New Orleans Saints, one yard short of the NFL record.

For the Saints to win consistently, however, they needed a lot of 55-yard field goals. New Orleans was struggling through another typically poor season when the Detroit Lions visited on Nov. 8, 1970. Saints head coach J.D. Roberts had just replaced Tom Fears after a 1-5-1 start, and the team was in turmoil. But in front of 30,000 empty seats at Tulane Stadium, New Orleans put up a fight. Dempsey, who had connected on only five of his first 15 attempts in 1970, kicked three field goals in the first three quarters, and the Saints led 16–14 in the fourth quarter. But with 11 seconds remaining, Detroit's Errol Mann booted an 18-yarder to put the Lions up by one point.

After the ensuing kickoff, quarterback Billy Kilmer moved the Saints near midfield, and the field goal team rushed out for a desperate attempt with two seconds left. With the holder crouched at the New Orleans 37-yard line, many Detroit players snickered. Some didn't even bother to rush the kick. They should have. "When Tom put his foot into the ball," said Saints' center Jackie Burkett, "it sounded like some kind of explosion." The ball cleared the cross bar by two feet, and the Saints won 19–17. The Saints would not win another game in 1970, and Dempsey was cut by New Orleans before the next season. But no kicker has bested his record in 32 years.

WHATEVER HAPPENED TO

Tom Dempsey kicked in the NFL for nine more years, retiring after his 1979 season with the Buffalo Bills. Though his career field goal percentage of 61.6 was mediocre at best, his celebrated record stood untouched for 28 years. In 1998 Denver's Jason Elam equaled Dempsey's mark of 63 yards in the thin air of Mile High Stadium. When he heard his record had been tied, Dempsey was one of the first to congratulate Elam.

After his playing days, Dempsey resettled in the town that made him famous, New Orleans. He became a successful car salesman and consultant, and managed a dealership. He now devotes much of his time to coaching youth football. The only words he won't tolerate from his 12- and 13-year-old players are "I can't."

Dempsey's last-second kick shattered the NFL record by seven yards.

22

GALE FORCE WINS

> *Gale Sayers tied the NFL record for touchdowns in a single game when he scored six times against the 49ers in 1965.*

For some football players, six touchdowns represent a solid season's work. But on a rainy December afternoon in 1965, Chicago's Gale Sayers scored that many touchdowns in a single game.

San Francisco's coaching staff had devised the "Chicago Defense" —stacking nine defenders on the line of scrimmage—to shut down the Bears' elusive rookie running back. Nevertheless, Sayers took a Rudy Bukich screen pass on Chicago's first possession and juked his way through San Francisco's defense and a muddy Wrigley Field for an 80-yard touchdown. "It seemed like everyone was slipping but me," said Sayers. He found the end zone twice more before halftime, scoring on running plays of 21 and seven yards.

In the second half, the Niners stubbornly stuck with their strategy of crowding the line, and on a third-and-one, Sayers burned them again with a 50-yard run off tackle for another touchdown. He capped the third quarter with a ho-hum one-yard TD plunge, but he saved his best for last. In the fourth quarter, he received a 49ers punt at his own 15, made a series of spins and cuts and ran 85 yards for his sixth and final score. With the Bears leading 54–20, Sayers was removed from the game, leaving him tied for the single-game league record. He had humiliated a defense specifically designed to stop him. "I just wonder how many Sayers would have scored if we hadn't set our defense to stop him," said Y.A. Tittle, one of the 49ers' assistant coaches.

During Chicago's 61–20 victory, Sayers carried the ball nine times, for 113 yards, and caught two passes, for 89 yards.

IN HIS CORNER

For four seasons Brian Piccolo was a sparingly-used halfback for the Bears. But in that short time he had a great impact on Gale Sayers and the Chicago Bears. When Sayers went down with a serious knee injury in 1968, it was Piccolo's friendship that helped him through his arduous recovery. Unfortunately, just as Sayers bounced back in 1969 to lead the league in rushing, his friend and roommate was stricken with cancer. Piccolo died of the disease the following year at age 26.

Up until the end, Sayers was there for his friend. When Sayers was presented with the league's most courageous football player award in 1969, he accepted it for Brian Piccolo. "Before Brian died there were only three things in the world that were important to me," Sayers said years later. "They were football, football and football. After that I realized how selfish I was. I felt I needed to adjust my life, to look around me, at my family, my friends and my future."

21

A BLAST FROM THE PAST

> *Two decades after a painful loss to Muhammad Ali, 45-year-old George Foreman won the heavyweight championship of the world.*

When George Foreman reappeared in 1987 after 10 years of self-imposed exile, the public hardly recognized him. Gone was the intimidating bruiser who had terrified the heavyweight division before falling to Muhammad Ali's rope-a-dope in Zaire in 1974. In his place was a smiling butterball of good humor, who pummeled a series of tomato cans while vying for another bid at the heavyweight title. Most of the boxing world looked upon him as a novelty act—sort of the senior citizen of the sweet science. But Foreman proved that he still had some gas in his tank when he went the distance with Evander Holyfield in 1991. Three years later, at 45, Foreman challenged the newly-crowned heavyweight champ Michael Moorer.

Foreman prepared for the fight in his usual manner—eating cheeseburgers and cracking jokes—but he was ready for the 26-year-old champ. For the first seven rounds, Moorer peppered Foreman with jabs and body shots, always making sure to avoid the old man's powerful right hand. Foreman became more aggressive in the eighth and ninth, but Moorer was still in control and led on all three judges' scorecards entering the 10th round. Perhaps feeling overconfident, Moorer decided to go toe-to-toe, and Foreman seized the opportunity. He landed a stinging left-right combination to Moorer's forehead that dropped the champ's hands and sent him back a step. Foreman finished Moorer off with a chopping right hand that left the champion sprawled across the canvas. The referee counted Moorer out, and Foreman knelt in prayer. Twenty years after his humiliating defeat in Zaire, he became the oldest heavyweight champion in boxing history.

In SI's Words

If you had known that all this time he had been driven by the defeat that had defined his career, would you have still found him amusing as he plodded, slowly for most of 10 rounds, after a newly vigorous Moorer? Would you have laughed then, bet against him then?

Or, instead, cautious of a shame Foreman would never let you guess at, would you have predicted that with a single right hand, driven downward with the shocking force of a hydraulic log-splitter and smack between the gloves of Moorer, he might redeem himself just like that? Well, you never know, do you? A guy can be 45 years old, and getting older in front of you, and be losing seven rounds of nine on two judges' scorecards, and, in a thunderbolt, he's suddenly reborn.

—RICHARD HOFFER, NOVEMBER 14, 1994

Knowing he needed a knockout to win, Foreman (near right) caught Moorer with a powerful right hand in the 10th round.

20

JORDAN RULES

> *Michael Jordan offered a glimpse of the future when he scored a playoff-record 63 points against the Boston Celtics in 1986.*

"He is the most awesome player in the NBA," raved Larry Bird. "Today in Boston Garden, on national TV, in the playoffs, he put on one of the greatest shows of all time." The 1986 Boston Celtics, destined for the franchise's 16th NBA championship, had just outlasted the Chicago Bulls in double overtime in Game 2 of the first round of the playoffs, but Bird was not describing one of his teammates. "I think he's God disguised as Michael Jordan," Bird said after Jordan scorched the Celtics for 63 points, an NBA playoff record.

Jordan would go on to win six NBA titles and five MVP awards, but on April 20, 1986, he was just a 23-year-old kid who had missed 64 games of the regular season with a broken foot. The Celtics, on the other hand, were one of history's great teams with Bird, Kevin McHale, Robert Parish, Bill Walton and Dennis Johnson.

Boston's gameplan for Game 2 was to shut down Jordan, who had scored 49 points in the opening game of the series, but covering him proved almost impossible. He scored 17 points in the first quarter and had 36 at the end of the third, when the Bulls led 91–88. "Being on the court with him," said teammate Orlando Woolridge, "you could tell there was something magical happening." The Celtics rallied in the fourth, and—with no time remaining—the Bulls needed two Jordan free throws to send the game into overtime. In the second overtime, Jordan's final basket evened the score at 131 and set a Boston Garden scoring record, but the Celtics scored the game's last four points for the win. "I'd give back all the points if we could have won the game," said Jordan. Two days later, Boston beat Chicago to sweep the series on their way to the title, but Jordan's performance hinted at the greatness to come.

In SI's Words

Then, in last week's 123–104 loss to the Celtics in Game 1, [Michael Jordan] sprang for 49, schooling the league's best defensive guard, Dennis Johnson, not to mention Rick Carlisle, Danny Ainge and Larry Bird, with dunks, floaters and long jumpers. He seemed to hang in the air longer than usual on his double-pumps and forays into the lane, as if to savor the sort of moments his long layoff had denied him. . . .

He scored over Bill Walton, Kevin McHale and Robert Parish when the Boston big men picked him up on switches, and on a steady stream of pull-up jumpers down the stretch. He even dropped in the tying free throws at the end of regulation while McHale classlessly goaded the crowd into trying to distract him. Jordan scored 63 in the game, a playoff record, eclipsing the mark of 61 set by L.A.'s Elgin Baylor in the same building in 1962.

—ALEXANDER WOLFF, MAY 28, 1986

Jordan connected on 22 of 41 field goal attempts and 19 of 21 free throws in his history-making performance.

19

HOW SWEDE IT IS

> *Shooting for perfection, Annika Sorenstam settled for history,*
> *becoming the first woman golfer to shoot a 59 in competition.*

When Annika Sorenstam dreamed of the perfect round of golf, she envisioned shooting a 54, 18 shots below par. Eighteen holes, 18 birdies. Mind you, the record score for any competitive round was 59 and no woman had ever shot better than 61, but that didn't stop Sorenstam. "That was just a way for me not to limit myself," she said, referring to her goal of 54.

That perfect round of 54 may remain beyond the grasp of Sorenstam—and any other human being—forever, but at the 2001 Standard Register Ping in Phoenix, she played the greatest round in women's golf history. In the second round, the 30-year-old Swede birdied her first eight holes and 12 of the first 13. She drilled all but one fairway and found every green, which allowed her steady putter to finish the job. When she sank a tricky 22-footer on her 11th hole, the tension became palpable. "It was like a pitcher with a no-hitter," said golfer Meg Mallon, who was paired with Sorenstam. "Nobody said a word so they wouldn't mess it up for her."

When she tapped in the final shot from six inches away, she leaped into her caddy's arms to celebrate the LPGA's first 59. "It was an easy 59," said Mallon. "She didn't even scare bogey out there." Her golf had been so precise that she putted for eagle or birdie on every hole. "I can't believe what I just did," said Sorenstam afterwards. Neither could her rivals. Kris Tschetter, who led the tournament after the first round, shot a respectable 69 and finished the day eight strokes behind. "What are you going to do when someone [else] shoots 59?" said golfer Pat Hurst. Start dreaming.

In SI's Words

When Annika Sorenstam became the first woman to break 60 in competition, shooting a 13-birdie, zero-bogey 59 during the second round of last week's Standard Register Ping in Phoenix, it was less a fluke than it was the inevitable result of this obsessive Swede's quest for perfection. In 2000 Sorenstam won five tournaments and finished second on the money list—and was so distraught she put herself through the most grueling off-season of her life. Sorenstam is not content to be merely great. Yes, at age 30 she has already qualified for the Hall of Fame, but over the past two years the balance of power on the LPGA tour has shifted to her archrival, Karrie Webb. "Annika is obsessed with being Number 1 again," says her husband, David Esch. . . .

What she did was play arguably the best round in golf history, even when compared with the six 59s that have been shot in men's competition, beginning with Al Geiberger's in 1977, a feat which earned him the nickname Mr. 59. Sorenstam benefited from no lucky shots or outrageous turns of fortune.

—*ALAN SHIPNUCK, MARCH 26, 2001*

Sorenstam's score of 27 under par for the
tournament was also a new LPGA record.

18

NOBODY'S PERFECT

> *No feat in sports history came to a more unsatisfactory conclusion than Harvey Haddix's 12 innings of perfect baseball in 1959.*

WHATEVER HAPPENED TO

Understandably, Harvey Haddix will always be remembered for his heartbreaking loss against the Braves in 1959. But fans may not recall that Haddix redeemed himself the following year, when he won two games, including the classic Game 7, in the 1960 World Series against the mighty New York Yankees.

With sluggers Mickey Mantle, Roger Maris and Yogi Berra leading the way, New York had won Games 2 and 3 by 16–3 and 10–0, respectively. Haddix limited the Yankee juggernaut to just two runs in Game 5, as the Bucs won 5–2. The Bronx Bombers exploded again in Game 6, routing Pittsburgh 12–0 to force a seventh game, which the Pirates, as baseball fans well know, won on a walk-off home run by Bill Mazeroski. Haddix, who had come on in relief in the ninth, was the pitcher of record.

Those were the moments—not the lost perfect game—that Haddix preferred to remember as his career highlights.

"Every single day I put on a uniform for the rest of my life," former Pittsburgh Pirates pitcher Harvey Haddix said during his retirement, "I was asked about the perfect game. Every single day."

And no wonder: On May 26, 1959, Haddix was perfect for 12 innings against the Milwaukee Braves, only to lose his bid for perfection—and the game—in the 13th. It was the Mona Lisa of pitching performances, until someone ripped the corner off the canvas before the artist could sign it.

Mixing his slider and fastball, Haddix silenced the bats of Hank Aaron, Eddie Mathews, Joe Adcock and the rest of the two-time defending NL champion Braves, who boasted a team batting average of .315. But Haddix's teammates couldn't scrape up a run against Milwaukee pitcher Lew Burdette, and at the end of nine the score was tied 0–0. Haddix had set down 27 batters in a row, yet had nothing to show for it.

He cruised through the 10th, 11th and 12th innings, and in the top of the 13th, the Pirates got another hit—their 12th of the game—but could not score. So Haddix, having retired 36 consecutive Milwaukee batters, trudged out to the mound for the 13th. Unlucky 13th, it turned out. The first batter, Felix Mantilla, rolled a grounder to third, and Pittsburgh's Don Hoak muffed the throw to first. Perfect game over. But Haddix still had a no-hitter, and a chance to win the game. The next batter, Mathews, sacrificed Mantilla to second. After intentionally walking Aaron, Haddix hung a 1–2 slider to Adcock. The Braves first baseman punched it over the fence in right center, permanently marring pitching's greatest masterpiece.

Haddix didn't realize he had been perfect until the game was over, when he told reporters it was "just another loss."

17

WOODEN SOLDIER

> *In the 1973 NCAA title game, UCLA's Bill Walton scored 44 points and nearly realized his coach's obsession with perfection.*

IN HIS CORNER

Bill Walton's performance on the basketball court was everything a coach could ask for, but his off-court interests and activities kept John Wooden up at night. "Between practices," Wooden said, "I had to worry about Bill."

Walton's liberal take on Vietnam, Watergate, drugs and long hair flew in the face of Wooden's straight-laced reputation. It wasn't as though Wooden discouraged his players from thinking for themselves, but he did demand that they accept the consequences of their actions. "He would say, 'I admire and respect your position,' " Walton said. " 'We'll miss you here at UCLA. We've enjoyed your time. Thanks for coming.' " Inevitably, Walton, or some other player with a gripe, shelved his cause and remained a Bruin. "His interest and goal was to make you the best basketball player but first to make you the best person," Walton said. In most cases, Wooden succeeded at both: His teams won 80 percent of their games, and 90 percent of his players graduated.

In the second half of the 1973 NCAA championship game against Memphis State, UCLA head coach John Wooden silently presided over his team's huddle during a timeout. Finally, Greg Lee asked Wooden if the Bruins should try some different plays. Wooden looked at his junior guard and replied, "Why?" Why, indeed. The one play that the Bruins had relied on all game had been unstoppable: get the ball to junior center Bill Walton.

The 1973 title game in St. Louis was the first to be televised in prime time, and a record viewing audience tuned in to watch UCLA, college basketball's reigning dynasty. The Bruins had won 74 consecutive games—35 straight in the NCAA tournament—but Memphis State thought they had a good chance if they could shut down Walton. "If he doesn't touch the ball, he can't score," Memphis State coach Gene Bartow told his Tigers. Memphis State fronted Walton in an effort to deny him the ball, but the strategy backfired. The Bruins simply lobbed passes to the 6' 11" redhead, who easily converted them into baskets. Still, Walton spent some of the first half on the bench with three fouls, and the Tigers shot well enough to reach halftime tied at 39. But UCLA and Walton exploded in the second half. The big man scored 14 points during a crucial 20–10 run, and the Bruins never looked back. When Walton left the game with a sprained ankle with 2:51 remaining, the game was no longer in doubt, and he had scored a championship game record 44 points. He had made 21 of 22 field goal attempts, and four other baskets were nullified as illegal dunks. "That was the best performance I've ever seen," Bartow said. "Ever."

Wooden called his 1973 team his best after Walton helped UCLA win its seventh straight NCAA title.

GO WITH THE FLO

> **Three months after shattering the world record for the 100 meters, Florence Griffith-Joyner swept the 100 and 200 at the 1988 Olympics.**

Her grin began at 70 meters, and when she crossed the finish line, her hands were already thrust skyward in celebration. Florence Griffith-Joyner ran away from the field at the 1988 Seoul Olympics and clocked the fastest 100 meters in Olympic history. "At that moment I knew everything was worth it," Griffith-Joyner said. "I felt so happy inside that I had it won I just had to let it out." Her gold medal-winning performance fell just short of her world record, but before the Games ended, Flo-Jo would cement her reputation as one of the greatest female sprinters in Olympic history.

Griffith-Joyner arrived in Seoul after a stunning performance at the U.S. Olympic Trials in Indianapolis, where she shattered the world record in the 100 meters by .27 seconds, the equivalent of 2½ yards. "I had the camera on her and she ran out of the picture," said Bob Kersee, who coached her during the trials. "I was stunned."

Her showing in Seoul proved that Indianapolis was no fluke, and her dominating performance in the Olympic 100 meters was a prelude to another world record. "This is the one I want more than any," Griffith-Joyner said. "The 200 gold and the record." She got both. Ninety minutes after setting a world record in the 200 semifinals, she bested it in the finals with a time of 21.34, nearly half a second better than the nine-year-old record. Needless to say, she won easily. "Words don't describe Florence," said American sprinter Gwen Torrence. "There are guys here who couldn't run 21.34." That's no exaggeration. Her time in the final would have beaten 36 of the 71 men who ran in the first round of the 200 meters.

After breaking the Olympic record twice during the preliminaries, Flo-Jo sailed to an easy victory in the 100 final.

IN HER CORNER

The 1988 Olympic track and field meet had all the makings of a family reunion. Florence Griffith-Joyner was coached by her husband, Al Joyner, a 1984 Olympic gold medalist in the triple jump. Joyner's sister and Flo-Jo's UCLA teammate, Jackie Joyner-Kersee, was a heavy favorite in the heptathlon and the long jump.

It wouldn't be a family reunion, though, without a little tension. Joyner-Kersee's husband, Bob Kersee, had coached Flo-Jo for eight years, but she began to train exclusively with her husband after the Olympic trials. "I wasn't hurt," Kersee said. "But I was really disappointed that Florence and I never communicated her problems."

If there was a feud, it didn't affect the women's performance. In addition to Flo-Jo's historic performance, Joyner-Kersee set a world record in the heptathlon and an Olympic record in the long jump. "Remember, no matter what we say, we all love each other," said Joyner-Kersee.

MAGIC SHOW

Filling in for the injured Kareem Abdul-Jabbar, Magic Johnson led the Lakers to victory in the decisive game of the 1980 NBA Finals.

Although the Lakers had won Game 5 of the 1980 NBA Finals to take a 3–2 lead against the 76ers, Los Angeles flew to Philadelphia lacking a favorite's confidence. The Lakers' star center Kareem Abdul-Jabbar had badly sprained his ankle and would not even make the trip. Sensing tension and concern among his teammates, 20-year-old rookie point guard Earvin (Magic) Johnson took Abdul-Jabbar's usual seat on the plane and announced, "Never fear, E.J. is here." Johnson would indeed fill Abdul-Jabbar's big sneakers and lead the Lakers to the title, demonstrating his superb all-around skills and versatility.

Coach Paul Westhead surprised everyone when he sent his 6' 9" point guard out to play center at the start of Game 6. Westhead, however, knew what he was doing. Losing the opening tip was practically the only thing Johnson did wrong. By halftime, Johnson had scored 22 points, grabbed eight boards and even launched a couple of Kareem-like hook shots, and the game was tied 60–60.

Johnson scored or assisted on 10 points during Los Angeles's 14–0 run to open the second half, and the Sixers never recovered. When the final buzzer sounded, Johnson had dominated the action from every position on the floor. He finished with a career-high 42 points—including a perfect 14 of 14 from the free throw line—15 rebounds, seven assists and three steals, and the Lakers won 123–107 for their first title in eight years. "I don't even know if Kareem could have done the things Magic did tonight," said Philadelphia's Julius Erving of the series' MVP. "The kid's a player."

Johnson became only the third man to win NCAA and NBA championships in back-to-back seasons.

WHATEVER HAPPENED TO

After playing on five championship teams and winning three MVP awards with the Lakers, Magic Johnson stunned fans in November 1991 when he announced that he had tested positive for the AIDS virus and was retiring from basketball. Though many took the news as something of a death sentence, Johnson educated both himself and others about his condition and has lived a healthy and productive life since his retirement.

Though semi-retired, he won a gold medal at the 1992 Olympics as a member of the original Dream Team. In 1995, at age 36, Johnson returned for one more stint with the Lakers. He played 32 games before retiring for good.

Since then, Johnson has taken his drive and determination to the world of business. Among his multimillion-dollar empire are a chain of movie theaters, Starbucks franchises, shopping plazas and a record label. "I got turned on when people said it's all over for Magic," said Johnson of his business success, "I wanted to show them I wasn't going away."

14

THE HUMAN LOCOMOTIVE

> *At the 1952 Olympics, Emil Zátopek of Czechoslovakia set Olympic records in the 5,000 meters, the 10,000 meters and the marathon.*

In the current era of increased specialization, no one is likely to attempt, let alone match, the feat that Emil Zátopek of Czechoslovakia accomplished at the 1952 Olympics. The wiry 29-year-old from northern Moravia won gold medals in the 5,000-meter run, the 10,000 and the marathon—a race he had never attempted before—in eight days' time.

He began with the 10,000 on Sunday, July 20. The defending Olympic champion in the event, Zátopek won it handily, defeating Alain Mimoun of France by nearly 16 seconds. He had a more difficult time in the 5,000 four days later, but he pulled away from the pack in the stretch—with his face twisted in its trademark grimace—and edged Mimoun again for the gold.

Lining up for the marathon the following Sunday, Zátopek decided to stay close to Jim Peters of Great Britain, the world record holder in the event, to make sure he was pacing himself properly. Nine miles into the race, Zátopek sidled up to Peters and asked him about the pace, which Zátopek deemed too fast. Bluffing, Peters told him the pace was too slow. "Are you sure?" Zátopek asked. "Yes," said Peters.

After pondering this in silence for a few miles, Zátopek ran past Peters and into the lead. By the 20-mile mark, Peters had dropped out with leg cramps and Zátopek was comfortably ahead of the pack. He entered the stadium more than two minutes ahead of his nearest competitor. With the huge crowd chanting "Zá-to-pek, Zá-to-pek," he broke the tape in an Olympic record time. The Jamaican relay team hoisted him to their shoulders and carried him around the stadium for a victory lap. Zátopek was the toast of Helsinki—and arguably the greatest distance runner of all time.

After settling for silver in the 5,000 meters at the 1948 Games, Zátopek came from behind to win gold in Helsinki.

WHATEVER HAPPENED TO

Emil Zátopek retired after the 1956 Olympics in Melbourne, where he finished sixth in the marathon. A national icon in Czechoslovakia, he finished his 17-year career with five Olympic medals, four of them gold, and 18 world records.

But when he signed the reform-minded *Manifesto of 2,000 Words* in 1968, his status as a hero was suddenly irrelevant. Moving in the following year, the Soviets crushed the growing reform movement, and Zátopek was dismissed from his senior position in the army and assigned a series of menial jobs. Proclaiming him "rehabilitated" in 1982, the government made him a translator of foreign sports journals for the national sports ministry.

Seven years later, the second Czech revolution restored Zátopek's rightful status, and he lived happily in Prague until November 2000, when he passed away at age 78.

A CHILD SHALL LEAD THEM

> *Brazil was only a minor soccer power until 17-year-old Pelé led them to the 1958 World Cup title in Sweden.*

He was born Edson Arantes do Nascimento, but the world would come to know him simply as Pelé. When he came to Sweden for the 1958 World Cup, though, that name meant nothing. At 17, he was the youngest player in the tournament. A knee injury kept him out of Brazil's first two games, and his early absence only fed the rumors that the great young talent from across the ocean was overrated.

When he finally debuted against the Soviet Union, he answered the skeptics by setting up Brazil's second goal in a 2–0 victory that advanced his team to the quarterfinals. In the single-elimination rounds, he dominated, scoring six of Brazil's 11 goals, He scored the game's only goal in the quarterfinal against Wales and three more in the 5–2 semifinal victory over France.

His last and most memorable two goals came in the final against Sweden. Brazil led at halftime 2–1, but the host Swedes had clamped down on Pelé. Ten minutes into the second half, though, Pelé broke loose. Standing with his back to the goal, he took a looping pass out of the air, flicked it over his defender and spun around to volley the ball into the goal. He scored the final goal of the game on a header, and Brazil won 5–2 to seize its first World Cup.

Brazil's victory helped make Pelé an international icon, a role he fulfilled for the rest of his life. His sublime grace on the field and his obvious love of the game made him the most recognized and celebrated player of the most popular sport in the world.

King Gustav VI of Sweden greeted Pelé before the 1958 World Cup final.

In SI's Words

In the semifinal Pelé unveiled all his skills. After France tied the game at one in the ninth minute—the first goal allowed by Brazil in the tournament—Pelé grabbed the ball out of the net and sprinted back upfield for the restart. There were still 81 minutes to play, and here was this teenager acting like a quarterback in a two-minute drill. "Let's go! Let's get started! Let's quit wasting time!" he shouted, waving his elder teammates into position. They stared at him, and then, together, they scored the next four goals, three of them by Pelé.

Before he completed his hat trick, Pelé was tackled viciously on his frail right knee. . . . Had Pelé retreated to the sideline, his team would have played with 10 men and the tackler would have been rewarded. Pelé would have none of that. Minutes later, when he saw the same defender closing in on him, Pelé flipped the ball over the villain's head—a "hat" move, as the Brazilians called it—scampered around him and blasted the ball into the net before it touched the ground.

—*IAN THOMSEN, NOVEMBER 29, 1999*

12

THE GALLOPING GHOST

> *In the first 12 minutes against Michigan in October 1924, Illinois's Red Grange shredded the Wolverines' defense for four touchdowns.*

On Oct. 18, 1924, a crowd of 67,000, including the nation's most famous sportswriters, filled Illinois's new football stadium to see how the Illini's All-America running back Red Grange would fare against Michigan's powerful defense. Michigan's coaching legend Fielding Yost was not impressed by Grange's credentials. "All Grange can do is run," he said dismissively. "All Galli-Curci can do is sing," answered Illini coach Bob Zuppke, referring to the renowned Italian opera singer. Before the day was done, Grange himself would have the final word.

He quickly dazzled the crowd by returning the opening kickoff 95 yards for a touchdown. One play after a Michigan fumble, he took the ball and scampered 67 yards down the sideline for another score. He returned the next Michigan punt 56 yards for a third touchdown. The next time he touched the ball, he galloped 45 yards for a fourth score, and the Illini led 28–0. And the game was only 12 minutes old.

Zuppke gave Grange a well-deserved break for the rest of the half, but the Ghost went back to work in the third quarter. He added another touchdown on a 13-yard dash and passed for a sixth touchdown in the fourth quarter. In 41 minutes of play, Grange ran for 402 total yards and passed for 64 more, as Illinois upset the Wolverines 39–14. Quite simply, it was the "most spectacular single-handed performance ever made in a major game," according to legendary coach Amos Alonzo Stagg. Members of the Michigan defense later admitted that they never laid a hand on Grange all afternoon, proving Grantland Rice's iconic words about Grange correct: "A streak of fire, a breath of flame/Eluding all who reach and clutch/A gray ghost thrown into the game/That rival hands may never touch."

Grange's heroics ended Michigan's 20-game unbeaten streak.

11

BACK IN THE SWING

Sixteen months after a near-fatal car accident, Ben Hogan rejuvenated his career with a victory at the 1950 U.S. Open.

Just when Ben Hogan thought he had mastered an unmasterable game, fate threw him a vicious curve. Months after he won his second PGA Championship, a car accident put his career and his life in jeopardy. Although he and his wife survived their collision with a Greyhound bus in February 1949, doctors doubted Hogan would ever walk again. But only 16 months later, Hogan braved agonizing leg pains to win the 1950 U.S. Open.

The accident had left Hogan with a broken pelvis, collarbone, ribs and ankle, and additional complications forced doctors to sever arteries in his leg. He spent two months in bed and his weight dropped to less than 100 pounds, but he never doubted he would recover. When two friends visited him immediately after the accident, he had them check his ruined car to see if his golf clubs were intact. They were, and Hogan vowed to put them to use as soon as possible.

His inspiring return began at the Los Angeles Open in January 1950. Limping around the course, Hogan tied Sam Snead, only to lose in a playoff. Five months later, at Merion Golf Club, he trailed by only two strokes after two rounds of the U.S. Open. But the 36 holes scheduled for Saturday promised to test Hogan's physical and mental endurance. He staggered around the course on weary legs, leaning on any shoulder he could grab. Hogan threatened to retire, but his caddie refused to let him, and a spectacular 210-yard 2-iron on the last hole salvaged a Sunday playoff. Refreshed after a night of rest, Hogan drained a 50-foot putt on the 17th hole of the playoff and won the championship. The victory helped Hogan win the golfer of the year award—despite playing in only four tournaments—and he went on to win five more majors in his career. "The 1950 Open was my biggest win," Hogan said in later years. "It proved I could still play."

In SI's Words

As a golfer Hogan was pure, not only because of the clean contact he made with the ball but also because he found fulfillment in the task. He possessed nobility and had soul. For all the outward severity of his manner and all the setbacks the game dealt him, any examination of Hogan reveals that he took profound pleasure in the physical and mental challenge of hitting wondrous golf shots. Hogan's aura was palpable, its own advertisement and something that inspired other players. Almost exclusively by actions instead of words, Hogan influenced more future greats than any 10 other golfers. . . .

For every emulator who made a mark, there have been hundreds of hard-practicing, flat-swinging, earnestly pronating, white-cap-wearing, no-talking perfectionists whose identification with every aspect of Hoganness allowed them to believe their failures were simply necessary steps on an inevitable, if very rocky, road to success. Hogan's methods and habits were such common knowledge, the jagged curve of his journey such an apparent blueprint, that it obscured the fact that genius can never be duplicated.

—*JAIME DIAZ, AUGUST 4, 1997*

Hogan's U.S. Open victory was just one of the eight majors he won between 1948 and 1953.

10

A PERFECT 10

Fourteen-year-old Nadia Comaneci of Romania stole the spotlight at the 1976 Montreal Games when she scored gymnastics' first 10.

IN HER CORNER

There is no Nadia Comaneci without Bela Karolyi, the burly Romanian gymnastics Svengali who discovered Comaneci when she was in kindergarten. Under his guidance, Comaneci became a gymnastics prodigy, and her success justified Karolyi's stern training methods. "We are not in the gym to be having fun," said Karolyi in later years. "The fun comes in the end, with the winning and the medals."

Karolyi defected to the United States in 1981 and established a gym in Houston, which attracted the best gymnasts in the country. Mary Lou Retton, who was one of those wide-eyed girls watching Comaneci on television in 1976, won the 1984 all-around gold medal under Karolyi's tutelage. His walrus mustache, broken English, and demonstrative cheerleading was almost as entertaining as Retton's heroics. Karolyi also coached the U.S. team to the 1996 Olympic gold medal in Atlanta. In 39 years of coaching, he has helped train nine Olympic and 15 world champions.

At the 1976 Olympics, a tiny, dark-eyed Romanian girl revolutionized women's gymnastics by creating a new standard of performance: perfection. Fourteen-year-old Nadia Comaneci earned the first perfect score, creating a historic moment for the sport, but the 86-pound wonder didn't stop there: She performed six more faultless routines, becoming the darling of the Montreal Games.

Comaneci's first perfect performance was on the uneven bars, but the crowd didn't know how to respond to the judges' score. The scoreboard, which hadn't been built with perfection in mind, could only muster a 1.0. For her part, Comaneci never had a doubt about her routine. "I knew it was flawless," she told reporters. "I have done it 15 times before."

The little girl with the stoic demeanor and fierce confidence was too honest to be modest. She had no reason to be modest. "She has three qualities," said her coach, Bela Karolyi. "The physical qualities—strength, speed, agility. The intellectual qualities—intelligence and the power to concentrate. And she has courage." Courage may have been her greatest asset. In contrast to the restrained elegance of previous Olympic gymnasts, Comaneci and her teammates threw themselves upon the various apparatuses with acrobatic flair. They risked life and limb with daring aerial maneuvers that were more athletic than balletic.

Comaneci performed four perfect routines on the uneven bars and three more on the balance beam. By the end of the Olympics, she had won three gold medals, a silver and a bronze, and irrevocably altered the future of her sport. Comaneci was the prototype of a new breed of female gymnast, and her dynamic performance inspired a generation of young girls.

Comaneci won the gold medal in the balance beam and led the Romanian team to the silver in the team competition.

DOUBLE VISION

> *At the 1996 Atlanta Games, Michael Johnson became the first man to win the 200 and 400 meters in the same Olympics.*

The 200 and 400 meters never have been considered tandem events. "There's always been a stereotype," said Michael Johnson. "If you ran the 200, you also ran the 100. If you ran the 400, that was all you did." Clearly, Johnson was no ordinary runner, and his double-gold performance at the 1996 Atlanta Games crowned him as the most consistent and versatile sprinter in track and field history.

Johnson's drive for the unprecedented double in Atlanta was fueled by his poor showing at the 1992 Games, when food poisoning spoiled his chances for a medal in the 200. He swallowed the disappointment and came back with a vengeance, winning 54 straight finals in the 400 and 21 straight in the 200. No runner had ranked No. 1 in the world simultaneously in the 200 and 400 meters; Johnson did for four years.

In Atlanta, Olympic organizers juggled schedules to allow Johnson to attempt his historic double, and he did not disappoint. Sporting a pair of custom-made gold sneakers, Johnson blazed to an Olympic record of 43.49 in the 400-meter final. Three nights later, in the 200-meter final, Johnson settled into the blocks before a raucous crowd of more than 80,000. "I live for that very moment in the blocks when you may win, but you don't know," Johnson said. Even he had no way of knowing what he was about to do. Crossing the finish line four yards ahead of the second-place runner, he leaped into the air at the number that greeted him on the clock: 19.32. "Nineteen-point-thirty-two," said Ato Boldon of Trinidad, who finished third. "That's not a time. It sounds like my dad's birth date." He had broken the world record by .34 seconds. "I am rarely shocked by my own performance," Johnson said. "And I'm shocked."

"I've always wanted to bring the two events together in a way that nobody else has ever done," said Johnson.

In SI's Words

Now he rose at the gun, stumbled slightly on his fourth step and then relaxed, putting himself into an ethereal zone. At 80 meters he accelerated with ungodly power. "I saw this blue blur," said [Ato] Boldon. "I thought, There goes first." [Frankie] Fredericks, who had ended Johnson's 21-race winning streak in Oslo in July 1996, was passed next. Then Johnson found a gear in which no man had run. "When you come off the turn into the straightaway, you can tell how fast you're going," Johnson said. "I knew I was running faster than I had ever run in my life."

Johnson's stride is a low, stiff-backed scamper, the subject of much study. But in the closing meters his knees seemed to float upward uncommonly, his feet sailing over the hard, orange surface. His facial features were twisted grotesquely, and at the line he glanced at the clock and then threw his arms toward the heavens. Boldon bowed in homage. Fredericks, whose 19.68 was the fastest 200 time ever by a man not named Michael, embraced Johnson and smiled as if acknowledging the folly of his chase.
—*TIM LAYDEN, AUGUST 2, 1996*

8

TWICE AS NICE

> *Four days after throwing a no-hitter against the Boston Braves, rookie Johnny Vander Meer did the same to the Brooklyn Dodgers.*

WHATEVER HAPPENED TO

"The no-hitters came too fast," Johnny Vander Meer said later in life. "I was just a kid who had done a freakish thing. I was more confused than thrilled." Although he finished 1938 with a 15–10 record, Vander Meer never found the control to harness his blazing fastball. He won only eight games in the next two seasons and even spent some time in the minor leagues.

He regained his form in 1941 and became a four-time All-Star while leading the National League in strikeouts in '41, '42 and '43. World War II cost Vander Meer two years of his prime, and he won more than 10 games in a season only once when he returned. He retired in 1951 with a 119–121 career record and a respectable 3.44 ERA. He managed briefly in Cincinnati's minor league system before leaving the game for a position with Schlitz brewing company. He retired to Tampa, Fla., the spring training home of the Reds, and passed away in 1997 at age 82.

There are only a handful of records in the baseball record book that can accurately be labeled unbreakable, and one of them belongs to an erratic southpaw of otherwise modest achievement named Johnny Vander Meer. As a rookie for the Cincinnati Reds in 1938, Vander Meer became the only man in baseball history to pitch two consecutive no-hitters. No other pitcher has ever thrown back-to-back no-hitters, and the odds of tossing three in a row are long indeed.

Vander Meer was a 23-year-old rookie with a 5–2 record when he faced the Boston Braves on June 11, 1938. Although his fastball was renowned both for its speed and inaccuracy, Vander Meer walked only three and struck out four in his 3–0 no-hitter against the Braves.

Four days later, a large crowd filled Brooklyn's Ebbets Field for Vander Meer's start against the Dodgers. Although the New Jersey native was coming off his finest performance, the big draw that evening was the debut of night baseball in New York. But Vander Meer quickly grabbed the spotlight by combining his scattershot aim with the park's dim lighting to keep the Dodgers off balance. "He was so wild," said Dodgers shortstop Leo Durocher, "you couldn't afford to dig in on him." Vander Meer walked five batters in the first eight innings, but he led 6–0 and still had not allowed a hit as he began the ninth. True to form, he walked the bases loaded before getting the last two outs. The bleachers emptied in celebration, and Vander Meer's teammates carried him off the field. Only eight pitchers in baseball history had pitched two no-hitters when Vander Meer threw his double no-no, and none of them had done it twice in a season. Vander Meer had done it twice in a week.

Vander Meer whiffed seven Dodgers during his second no-hitter.

7

THE MAGICAL MILE

> **In 1954 Roger Bannister ran the first sub-four-minute mile, shattering a mythic barrier that experts thought might never be breached.**

The four-minute mile was, and remains, among the most prominent milestones in sports history. It wasn't considered a realistic proposition until Jules Ladoumegue of France broke 4:10 in 1931. Several other runners followed him through that barrier, but the four-minute mile still lay on the distant horizon of possibility. Australian miler John Landy called it "a brick wall." Others equated breaking it to being the first to conquer Mt. Everest.

When England's Roger Bannister toed the starting line at Oxford's Iffley Road track on May 6, 1954, the current world record of 4:01.4 had stood for nine years. If the wind hadn't died down on that damp spring evening, it may have remained standing for another day. Bannister waited until 20 minutes before his race—anxiously watching the flag atop a church across the street—before deciding that the attempt was on.

His teammates Chris Brasher and Chris Chataway acted as his "rabbits," maintaining a pace of 60-second quarter miles. They led Bannister through the half-mile in 1:58.3. He hit the bell lap in 3:00.5, still trailing Chataway. On the backstretch he opened up his stride and took the lead, pulling farther and farther away from the pack. Barreling alone down the stretch, he later wrote, "My body had long since exhausted all its energy, but it went on running just the same."

With the crowd on its feet, Bannister crossed the line in 3:59.4. "Bannister's performance," wrote the *Times* of London the next day, "will earn for him athletic immortality no matter how soon someone else goes a fraction of a second better."

Of course the paper was right: Nearly 50 years later, few remember that Landy ran 3:58.0 only 46 days after Bannister's historic performance. The brick wall had already been smashed.

In SI's Words

[Bannister] does not dwell in the past but will wax eloquent on it when called upon to do so. "When I went up to Oxford, I wanted to take part in sport," he said. "I was too light for rowing, and I wasn't skilled enough for rugby. But I knew I could run. . . .

"I suppose people will remember me for [the four-minute mile]," he said. "But my life has other strands."

Indeed. *The Four Minute Mile*, which Bannister wrote in six weeks as a 26-year-old medical student, remains one of the best sports books you'll ever read. As chairman of the British Sports Council, he instituted track's first drug-testing program, in 1973. Bannister retired last October after eight years as Master of Oxford's Pembroke College, but he hardly plans to be inactive: He will edit medical journals and revise the third edition of his *Disorders of the Autonomic Nervous System*. He's 65 now and walks with a cane after breaking his right ankle in a car accident in '75. But he still gets exercise, by cycling.

—MERRELL NODEN, JANUARY 31, 1994

"Those last few seconds seemed never ending,"
wrote Bannister of his historic feat.

6

ICE AND EASY

> *Eric Heiden set Olympic records in five events as he swept the speed skating competition at the 1980 Lake Placid Games.*

A fresh-faced 21-year-old from Madison, Wisc., Eric Heiden had already become the first male speed skater to win four gold medals in one Olympics, winning gold in the 500, the 1,000, the 1,500 and the 5,000 meters at the 1980 Winter Games. There was one speed skating event left, the 10,000 meters, but Heiden was not about to let the race get in the way of a good time. Rather than check in early on the eve of the race, he joined friends for the U.S.-U.S.S.R. medal-round hockey game, in which two of Heiden's hometown buddies were playing.

As every sports fan and the vast majority of Americans know, the U.S. team made history that night in Lake Placid, and their David-and-Goliath victory got Heiden so worked up that he had a mild case of insomnia. He overslept the next morning and had to scramble to get to the track, gobbling a few slices of bread for breakfast as he left the Olympic village.

He made it in time, though, to carve a permanent place for himself in the annals of Olympic glory. Racing in the second pair, Heiden, who had set four Olympic records already, broke the world record in the 10,000 by more than six seconds.

"I didn't get into skating to be famous," Heiden said. "If I wanted to be famous, I would have stuck with hockey." His protestations aside, Heiden's name continues to resonate. In those nine days of brilliance at Lake Placid, he became the first, and remains the only, person in history to win five individual gold medals at a single Olympics.

In 2000 the Associated Press named Heiden its male Winter Olympic Athlete of the Century.

In SI's Words

Not since Secretariat obliterated the 1973 Belmont field by 31 lengths had a champion completed a sweep with such decisiveness. Skating the 25-lap, 6.2-mile race in 14:28.13, Heiden had sliced 6.20 seconds off the world record and beaten his closest rival, Piet Kleine of the Netherlands, by 7.90 seconds—the equivalent of 100 meters. In a sport of benumbing repetition, Heiden, the greatest speed skater in history, had managed to add an element of surprise by making his final triumph such a runaway. . . .

For sporting purposes, he should perform with one ice skate and one moon boot. When Levi's was outfitting the American team before the opening ceremonies, the only pair of pants that would fit over Heiden's 29-inch thighs had a 38-inch waist, which is six inches bigger than he needs. "It's not exciting to be skating right now," said Frode Rönning, the Norwegian bronze medalist in the 1,000. "The medals are delivered before the race."

—E.M. SWIFT, MARCH 3, 1980

5

TALL TALE

Wilt Chamberlain's 100-point game in 1962 may have seemed like a fairy tale, but it was real—just ask the New York Knicks.

Our first task in preparing this book was to define the word "feat." It has an old-world, almost circus-like feel, evoking mustachioed strongmen as much as, say, Michael Jordan. There are dozens—we came up with more than 60—of sporting accomplishments that fall under the rubric of a great feat, but we agreed that none fits the term better than Wilt Chamberlain's record 100-point game for the Philadelphia Warriors against the New York Knicks in 1962.

Like a giant under the big top, Chamberlain towered over the Knicks that night, scoring slightly more than a basket a minute. He also demonstrated concentration worthy of the high wire—normally a poor free throw shooter, he hit 28 of 32 from the line that night. And as he approached 100 points, he showed the poise of a ringmaster, deftly handling the pressure of the frenzied crowd and of his opponents, who had abandoned their goal of winning the game in favor of a single-minded determination to prevent Chamberlain from topping the century mark. This effort included stalling, fouling Chamberlain's teammates at every chance and double- and triple-teaming the big man. Chamberlain still hit 100, scoring his final bucket with just under a minute to play.

That moment, though, was as rife with tension as an exchange on the flying trapeze. Chamberlain missed two shots, but Warriors forward Ted Luckenbill was there to grab the rebound each time. After the second miss, Luckenbill passed to forward Joe Ruklick near the sideline. As the clock ticked down past 50 seconds, New York guard Rich Guerin ran at Ruklick, intent on fouling him to prevent Chamberlain from getting another shot at 100. Too late; Chamberlain spun away from his man and toward the basket. Ruklick flipped the ball to him and the Big Dipper dropped in a finger roll. Like so many human

Chamberlain led the league in scoring in 1961–62 with an NBA-record 50.4 points per game.

cannonballs, the spectators thronging the court burst forth and exploded onto the hardwood, stopping the game with 46 seconds on the clock, to celebrate Wilt's 100.

If these elements weren't enough to enhance the feat's atmosphere of carnival wonder, consider that in an effort to reach new fans the NBA had scheduled the game in Hershey, Pa., where the air smells like chocolate and the arena sits in the middle of an amusement park. And there were no television cameras, few photographers and only 4,124 patrons on hand to bear witness to the wondrous feat, which is preserved mainly in the memories of fans, where all great feats shine brightest.

Chamberlain left the game after his last basket (above), keeping the record at an even 100 points. "That round number of 100 is magical," said teammate Al Attles.

4

MAKING A SPLASH

> *Mark Spitz won seven gold medals and set seven world records at the 1972 Olympics before the Games were marred by terrorism.*

IN HIS CORNER

Mark Spitz hated losing. His father, Arnold, told him at an early age that "Swimming isn't everything; winning is." To Spitz, it was better not to enter an event at all than to enter and not win.

The 100-meter freestyle at the 1972 Olympics promised to be Spitz's most competitive event of the Games, and he debated withdrawing from the race rather than risk defeat. But Spitz's longtime personal coach, Sherm Chevoor, warned his star pupil, "They'll say you're chicken, that you're afraid." Chevoor knew that the only thing Spitz despised more than losing was being labeled a coward. Spitz thought it over, and decided to stay in the race. He went wire-to-wire, holding off teammate Jerry Heidenreich at the finish to pick up his sixth gold medal of the Games.

Swimming the butterfly leg on the U.S. men's 4 x 100-meter medley relay, Mark Spitz won an unprecedented seventh gold medal at the 1972 Olympics in Munich. When the race ended, his teammates hoisted him onto their shoulders and paraded him around the pool in celebration of arguably the greatest performance in the history of the Games. Spitz had not only won seven gold medals (in the 100- and 200-meter freestyles, the 100- and 200-meter butterflies, and three relays), he had also set seven world records.

That victory lap, Spitz said, meant more to him than the famous poster he posed for, wearing only his Speedo and his gold medals, an image that became the highest-selling sports poster of all time. But Spitz had little time to enjoy his historic moment, for only hours after his last race, Palestinian terrorists invaded the Olympic Village, kidnapped 11 Israeli athletes. The horrifying siege and the deadly confrontation that followed cast a dark shadow over Spitz's golden feat.

Indeed, Spitz, who is Jewish, left Munich immediately after the terrorists struck. "It was kind of unbelievable," he said. "It was terrible." And it was diabolically, and diametrically, opposed to the Olympic spirit Spitz had embodied with his tremendous feat. Of his seven races, only the 100- and 200-meter freestyles were close; Spitz's teams won their three relays by an average of 4.4 seconds—a huge margin in swimming. Just like Spitz's lead over most athletes in the annals of Olympic glory.

Spitz's performance in Munich redeemed his "poor" showing at the '68 Games, when he won only two gold medals.

In SI's Words

Secretariat ran flat into legend, started right out of the gate and never stopped, ran poor Sham into defeat around the first turn and down the backstretch and sprinted clear, opening two lengths, then four, then five. He dashed to the three-quarter pole in 1:09.45, the fastest six furlong clocking in Belmont history. I dropped my head and cursed Turcotte: What is he thinking about? Has he lost his mind? The colt raced into the far turn, opening seven lengths past the half-mile pole. The timer flashed his astonishing mark: 1:34⅕!

He came home alone. . . . As rhythmic as a rocking horse, he never missed a beat. . . . The clock flashed crazily: 2:22, 2:23. The place was one long, deafening roar. The colt seemed to dive for the finish, snipping it clean at 2:24.

I bolted up the press box stairs with exultant shouts and there yielded a part of myself to that horse forever.

—WILLIAM NACK, JUNE 4, 1990

"A TREMENDOUS MACHINE"

> *Secretariat capped horse racing's most memorable Triple Crown with a 31-length victory at the 1973 Belmont.*

In the spring of 1973 a splendid colt offered a world-weary public a glimpse of pure greatness. Secretariat's pursuit of horse racing's elusive Triple Crown captured the imagination of a country haunted by Watergate and Vietnam. The country needed a hero, and it found it in a chestnut-colored horse with a giant heart. "Imagine the greatest athlete in the world," said Seth Hancock, owner of Claiborne and Stone Farms, where Secretariat retired. "Now make him the perfect height. Make him real intelligent and kind. And on top of that, make him the best-lookin' guy ever to come down the pike. Secretariat was all those things in a horse."

When Secretariat won the Kentucky Derby and the Preakness Stakes—the first two legs of the Triple Crown—his performances amazed even those who had predicted greatness for the colt when he was the Horse of the Year as a two-year-old. At the Derby, he rallied from last place to win in record time, 2½ lengths in front of his closest rival. Two weeks later, in Baltimore, Secretariat won again by 2½ lengths, and only a clock malfunction prevented him from breaking another official race record.

Only the Belmont Stakes stood between Secretariat and the first Triple Crown in 25 years. Seventy thousand fans packed Belmont Park as Secretariat and four other horses were led to the gate on the first Saturday in June. Secretariat shared the early lead with Sham, who had finished second in the Derby and the Preakness, but the pace quickened as they neared six furlongs. Secretariat pulled away, and his trainer, Lucien Laurin, worried that the horse wouldn't last. The lead, however, continued to widen—14 . . . 15 . . . 16 . . . 17 lengths—as Secretariat reached the third turn. "Every time I looked up, Secre-

Secretariat would have trounced Gallant Man, the previous Belmont record holder, by 13 lengths.

"He was running on his own," said Turcotte (above). "If I asked him to go harder through the stretch, I don't know how fast he would have gone."

tariat looked smaller and smaller," said jockey Angel Cordero Jr., who was aboard third-place finisher My Gallant. The roar of the crowd welcomed Secretariat as he thundered home. Finally, jockey Ron Turcotte could no longer resist. "I just had to turn around," he said. "I kept hearing the announcer saying how far ahead we were, and I had to look for myself." There was no horse within 31 lengths when Secretariat crossed the finish line in a time of 2:24, 2⅗ seconds faster than the track record. Secretariat had won not only the Triple Crown, but also the hearts of a nation and a permanent place in racing history.

Laurin (near right) and owner Penny Tweedy (far right) celebrated Secretariat's Belmont victory.

"At the half-mile pole," said Turcotte, "I realized I couldn't hear any horses behind me."

AFTERNOON DELIGHT

Jesse Owens broke or tied six world records in a span of 45 minutes at the 1935 Big Ten Conference track and field championships.

In the late 1990s the United States Postal Service issued a series of stamps commemorating historical and cultural touchstones from the 20th century. Celebrating the landmark accomplishments of such icons as Franklin Delano Roosevelt, Elvis Presley and Jackie Robinson, the series spotlighted 15 figures for each decade. Jesse Owens was honored in the set of stamps for the 1930s, but not, as one might assume, for his four-gold-medal performance at the 1936 Olympics in Berlin. No, Owens was singled out for his equally astounding, but lesser-known, feat at the Big Ten championships one year earlier. Competing for Ohio State University on a sunny May afternoon in Ann Arbor, Mich., Owens broke five world records and tied a sixth in a span of 45 minutes.

At 3:15 Owens ran away from the field in the 100-yard dash to tie the world record of 9.4 seconds. Ten minutes later he made one attempt in the long jump, leaping 26' 8¼", which was not only good enough to win the event but was also a world record that stood for 25 years. At 3:45, Owens broke the world record in the 220-yard dash by three-tenths of a second, clocking 20.3. He won by 10 yards, and was also given credit for breaking the 200-meter dash world record along the way. At 4:00 Owens became the first man to break 23 seconds for the 220-yard hurdles, blitzing the field in 22.6. He also broke the 200-meter hurdles record en route. "In the space of 45 minutes," said Owens's Ohio State teammate Charlie Beetham, "he put on the most outstanding track and field performance of all time." Sixty-seven years after the fact, no one would dispute that claim.

One month after his record-breaking afternoon in Ann Arbor, Owens won four events at the NCAA championships.

IN HIS CORNER

Born in Danville, Ala., in 1913, Jesse Owens was the 10th child of Henry and Mary Owens. The family moved to Cleveland, Ohio, when Jesse was nine years old, and it was in that industrial city by the shores of Lake Erie that his athletic career took root. While a student at Fairmount Junior High, Owens came under the tutelage of Charles Riley, the school's track coach. "He was the first white man I ever knew," said Owens, "and without ever trying, he proved to me beyond all proof that a white man can understand—and love—a negro."

Riley recognized Owens's rare talent and, after learning that Owens had to work each afternoon following school, agreed to meet him on weekday mornings for workouts on the track. He helped shape Owens's values and inspired him to aim for great things. Owens called Riley "Pop" and later in his life said that Riley was "a rare man, as much a father to me as Henry Owens was."

1

RARE AIR

Bob Beamon leaped into history in Mexico City in 1968, obliterating the world record in the long jump by nearly two feet.

WHATEVER HAPPENED TO

As he stood on the podium to receive his Olympic gold medal, Bob Beamon thought, Where do I go from here?

He had produced what has become one of the most iconic moments in sports history, but he knew that repeating his Olympic performance would be all but impossible. Then, injuries curtailed his career, and an Olympic comeback in 1972 fell short.

Since retiring, Beamon has dedicated himself to philanthropic efforts around the world. He currently serves as the chairman of Bob Beamon Communications, where he has worked with *Fortune* 500 companies as a corporate spokesperson and served as a management consultant to various other companies.

His record withstood Carl Lewis's pursuit, and many in the sport thought the mark would last into the 21st century. But in 1991, in an effort worthy of Beamon himself, Mike Powell jumped almost a foot farther than he ever had before and beat the record with a leap of 29' 4¼" inches in Tokyo.

Bea·mon·esque *adj.* describing a superior athletic achievement that dwarfs all previous efforts. *See 1968 Olympic Games.*

Bob Beamon was an unlikely candidate for linguistic immortality when he entered the Olympic Stadium in Mexico City on Oct. 18, 1968. Six months earlier, the University of Texas–El Paso had taken his scholarship away after he boycotted a track meet against Brigham Young because of the Morman school's racial policies. He still qualified for the Olympics, but his performances had been inconsistent, and he wasn't considered the best jumper on the U.S. team.

The high altitude of Mexico City created ideal jumping conditions, and Olympic officials were optimistic that the competition might yield the first-ever 28-foot jump. Since Jesse Owens had set it at 26' 8¼" in 1935, the long jump record had been tied or broken eight times, yet only increased by 8½ inches. Beamon's teammate Ralph Boston and the Soviet Union's Igor Ter-Ovanesyan had traded the record back and forth and hoped to set another in Mexico City. Beamon, however, stole their thunder immediately.

In his first jump in the finals, he launched himself through the air and almost out of the long jump pit. "I knew I made a great jump," said Beamon. When the official distance was announced, a shock wave shook the stadium. Beamon not only became the first man to jump 28 feet—a distance no other man would reach for 12 years—but he had also surpassed 29 feet. His leap of 29' 2½" shattered the record by 21¾ inches. "Compared to this jump, we are as children," said Ter-Ovanesyan. The competition was essentially over; no one came within two feet of Beamon's astonishing jump.

Beamon never jumped even 27 feet again in his career, but his record would last for 23 years. His contribution to track and field history, and the English language, would last much longer.

"I was training to jump 27 feet, maybe 28 feet," said Beamon. "But I never dreamed of 29 feet."

SPECTACULAR SEASONS

INTRODUCTION

Sports are measured in seasons—the building blocks of careers that ultimately lead to the Hall of Fame, Palookaville, or somewhere in between. Some of the spectacular seasons described in this chapter were indicative of a lifetime of excellence. Others represent the summit of an otherwise pedestrian career. Either way, the athletes who produced these seasons so dominated their game during a particular chapter of their career that their supremacy was undeniable, and their names are permanently linked to a certain year, record or number.

Baseball, as every rotisserie leaguer will attest, is all about numbers, and the home run is the game's greatest attraction, so it is no surprise that home run hitters appear twice on our list of sport's 10 greatest single-season feats. Simple arithmetic says that the 73 home runs Barry Bonds launched in 2001 are greater than the 54 Babe Ruth clob-

bered in 1920, but you might be surprised where we rank Bonds and the Bambino. One of Ruth's contemporaries, Hack Wilson, set one of baseball's most enduring records in 1930, when he drove in 191 runs. Even in today's game, which is played in smaller ballparks by bigger players, no one has come within 21 runs of the record in 64 years. Wilson is a perfect example of a performer who might have slipped into obscurity if not for his astounding feat in 1930. Similarly, pitcher Denny McLain might have been remembered only for his rebelliousness as a player—and lawlessness as an ex-player—had he not won 31 games in 1968.

Greatness has a way of rising to the top—and it seems to get there even faster when it is unappreciated at first. There have never been two more disparate personalities than Maurice Richard and Barry Sanders, but both men overcame doubts about their physical ability to dominate their

Bonds's season was one of the greatest individual achievements of all time, but Miami and Manchester won historic titles.

respective sports. Richard, who had been labeled too brittle for hockey after a series of early injuries, proved his mettle in 1944–45 when he scored 50 goals in 50 games. While the Rocket bristled with intensity, Sanders was a humble, soft-spoken man. But he, too, proved the skeptics wrong. Many observers considered him too small for Division I football, but after two years as a back-up, Sanders exploded for 2,628 yards and 39 touchdowns as a junior at Oklahoma State.

These are the seasons we celebrate in the following pages: the performances that have taken up permanent residence in the minds of most sports fans. And again, they can often be expressed as iconic numbers, like 17–0. Every pro football fan knows that that was the Miami Dolphins record in 1972, when, under the stern guidance of coach Don Shula, they beat all comers in the NFL. They capped their perfect season—the only one in league history—with a 14–7 win over Washington in Super Bowl VII. Twelve years later, Shula's hopes rested on the ability of a single player: Dan Marino. The young Pittsburgh native with the curly hair enjoyed one of the greatest seasons by a quarterback in NFL history and led Miami to another Super Bowl.

This chapter features a famous triple—Manchester United's historic 1999 season, when the club won the Premiership, the FA Cup and the European Champions League—and a triple-double, which Cincinnati point guard Oscar Robertson averaged during the 1960–61 NBA season. That's right, the Big O averaged 31 points, 12 rebounds and 11 assists a game that year.

But however they are signified, and regardless of whether the performance was the exception or the rule for a given athlete or team, each season you'll read about in this section lives up to the chapter heading.

10

MANCHESTER'S MIRACLE

> *Moments from defeat, Manchester United stunned Bayern Munich to become the first English team to win the "Triple."*

"I kept saying to myself, 'Keep your dignity and accept it is not your year,' " said Manchester United manager Alex Ferguson, remembering his thoughts as his team trailed Bayern Munich 1–0 with time winding down in the 1999 European Champions League final.

The game had entered stoppage time, and it seemed clear that Man U's season would be merely outstanding, falling just shy of historic. The club had won the Premier League and the F.A. Cup, but the Champions League title, alas, would get away.

A great year, yes, but Ferguson's disappointment was understandable. All season long the Red Devils had embodied that oldest of sports clichés, the Team of Destiny. Down 2–0 to Juventus in the Champions League semifinals, Man U had rallied to win 3–2. Trailing Tottenham by a goal on May 16, United scored twice to clinch the Premier League title on the final day of the season.

Only three teams in soccer history had accomplished the hallowed "Triple" of winning the Champions League along with their domestic league and cup titles, and none of them was English. United could be—*had* to be, after coming so close, overcoming so much—the first. But now, time was running out. While Ferguson grappled with his emotions on the sideline, Man U striker Teddy Sheringham whistled a shot from the top of the box and into the lower corner to tie the game. Bayern Munich fans had scarcely comprehended the equalizer when Reds striker Ole Gunnar Solskjaer provided the winner, blasting a loose ball off a corner kick into the top of the net. In a two-minute span, Man U's 1999 season hurtled from outstanding to legendary.

EPILOGUE

Manchester United did not repeat its historic triple the following season, but it did defend its Premier League title—the club's sixth such championship in eight years. If U.S. sports fans need a point of reference to understand Manchester's legacy, they need look no further than the New York Yankees, the Man U of baseball. Both clubs have storied histories and a string of recent successes, both clubs are fabulously wealthy and spend lavishly to acquire the best talent available, and both clubs seem to attract as much enmity as adulation. In fact, the Yankees and United have so much in common that they formed a global marketing partnership in early 2001. The rich get richer, it seems.

Solskjaer, who came off the bench late in the game against Bayern, celebrated his title-clinching goal in the 93rd minute.

9

MR. McLAIN'S WILD RIDE

> **Denny McLain's career was derailed by arm injuries and poor judgment, but his 31-win season of 1968 may never be repeated.**

"There's never been any like Denny McLain," said Ernie Harwell, voice of the Detroit Tigers. Indeed, McLain marched to the beat of a different drummer. The cocky righthander's dominance on the mound in the late 1960s was often overshadowed by his moonlighting as a musician, his jetsetting around the celebrity circuit and his numerous run-ins with team and league authorities. But in 1968, he was best known for his pursuit of 30 victories.

Pitchers dominated the 1968 season. Bob Gibson tossed 13 shutouts and had a 1.12 ERA, and the American League's batting champion, Carl Yastrzemski, hit only .301. But McLain was the sport's undeniable star, and no one knew it better than McLain. "When you can do it out there between the lines, you can live any way you want," he said, as he tested the limits of his growing celebrity. "Our manager had one set of rules for Denny and another set for the 24 other guys on our team," said McLain's teammate Mickey Lolich. As long as he won, McLain had a long leash. And in 1968, he won 31 times, lost just six and led the Tigers to the pennant. McLain pitched 28 complete games and was the runaway winner of the American League Cy Young Award.

While McLain was not the first pitcher to win 30 games in a season, he might be the last. Five-man rotations and a greater emphasis on relief pitching has made the milestone seemingly unreachable. That's not to say that 30 wins was ever easy. When McLain chased the mark, no pitcher had won 30 games since St. Louis's Dizzy Dean in 1934. Since McLain, no pitcher has won more than 27, making the Motor City "Mighty Mouth" the only pitcher to accomplish the feat in 68 years.

McLain started three games in the 1968 World Series and pitched a complete game to win Game 6.

OKLAHOMA STAMPEDE

Barry Sanders set NCAA single-season records for rushing yards and touchdowns in his only season as a starter at Oklahoma State.

Forces of nature are difficult to predict and impossible to control. The same could have been said about a tornado-like tailback named Barry Sanders. In 1988 the 5' 8", 197-pound Oklahoma State junior touched down on the football field and proceeded to chew up yardage, break long touchdowns runs and lay waste to the NCAA record books.

After rushing for only 947 yards as a backup in the first two years of his college career, Sanders began his junior year with a bang: In the Cowboys' season opener against Miami of Ohio, he returned the opening kickoff 100 yards for a touchdown. Before the game was over, he added 178 yards and two more scores. Lest anyone think that performance was a fluke, Sanders ripped through the rest of the schedule. He torched Tulsa for 304 yards and five TDs, ran for 312 yards and five scores against Kansas and carried the ball a season-high 44 times for 332 yards and four touchdowns in Oklahoma State's season finale against Texas Tech. Like a Tasmanian Devil inside a pinball machine, he spun, bounced and juked his way around beleaguered defenders. "He is quick and can make people miss him, and he can run over people in the open field," said Oklahoma coach Barry Switzer. "Oklahoma State didn't block us and Sanders [still] gained 215 yards on us."

Sanders finished the season with 2,628 yards rushing and 39 touchdowns, both new NCAA records. He easily won the Heisman Trophy and fired a parting shot by galloping for 222 yards and five touchdowns against Wyoming in the Holiday Bowl. Rather than attempt to repeat his zero-to-hero junior season, the sudden superstar entered the NFL Draft in search of other defenses to terrorize.

Sanders ran for 174 yards and four touchdowns in Oklahoma State's 41–21 win against previously undefeated Colorado.

EPILOGUE

Barry Sanders was selected third overall by the Detroit Lions in the 1989 NFL Draft, and it didn't take him long to become one of the premier backs in the league. As a rookie, he rushed for 1,470 yards and 14 touchdowns, and in 1991 he led Detroit to a 12–4 record and their first playoff appearance since 1983. Though the Lions failed to reach the Super Bowl during his career, Sanders gained more than 1,000 yards in each of his first 10 seasons and became only the third back to top 2,000 yards in a season in 1997. He seemed on course to break Walter Payton's career rushing mark of 16,726 yards, when he abruptly retired in 1999. Never one to dwell on numbers, individual awards or accolades, Sanders ended his professional career as the league's second all-time leading rusher (15,269 yards).

7

ROCKET'S RED GLARE

> *Fast and fiery, Montreal's Maurice Richard scored 50 goals in 50 games in 1944–45 and fueled the rise of a sports dynasty.*

EPILOGUE

Maurice Richard's line went 1-2-3 in scoring in the NHL in 1944–45, and the Canadiens easily won the regular-season title. But when the playoffs began, the Toronto Maple Leafs, who barely cracked .500 during the regular season, ignored Montreal's formidable credentials. Although Richard scored six goals in the opening round series, giving him 56 goals in 56 total games, it was not enough. After taking the first two games of the series, the Leafs held on to eliminate the Canadiens in six games.

But Montreal and Richard would bounce back, to say the least. Before he retired in 1960, the Rocket and Montreal won seven more Stanley Cups, including five in a row to close out his career. He retired as the league's alltime leading goal scorer, and his record of six overtime playoff goals still stands. In 1999 the NHL established a new award, the Maurice Richard Trophy, which is presented to the league's top goal scorer each season.

"When he is worked up, his eyes glow like headlights," said Montreal Canadiens' general manager Frank Selke. "It's not a glow but a piercing intensity. He is a frightening sight."

Maurice (Rocket) Richard terrorized opponents in an era of jagged scars, black-and-blues and toothless grins. No player combined the skill and ruggedness of the age better than Richard. Goaltenders would pray to a higher power before games with Richard's Canadiens, and rivals boasted of the bruises he tattooed on their bodies.

During the 1944 playoffs, Richard had teased the league with a glimpse of his potential, exploding for 12 goals in nine playoff games to lead the Canadiens to the Stanley Cup. In 1945, the 23-year old Rocket engaged his turbo boosters. He scored 15 goals in one nine-game stretch. He scored five in one game. He produced 10 multiple-goal games during the season, and he entered the last game of the year, against the Boston Bruins, with 49 goals. That total already had broken the single-season record by five goals, but 50 goals in 50 games, well, that would be a landmark figure. Pressure? Not for the single-minded Rocket; he beat Harvey Bennett for his 50th goal of the year with less than three minutes left in the third period.

Fifty goals immediately became hockey's Holy Grail, and although his single-season goal record was broken in 1966 by Bobby Hull, it wasn't until the league expanded and the schedule was extended that another player equaled Richard's mark of 50 goals in 50 games. When Mike Bossy of the New York Islanders tied the record in 1981, the Rocket's red glare was still smoldering. "He was a little mad," Bossy said. "He grabbed me by the neck for the cameras . . . and was squeezing me pretty tight."

During Richard's historic 1944–45 season, he never went more than two games without scoring a goal.

6

A GIANT AMONG MEN

> **In an era of power hitters, no slugger packed more punch than Barry Bonds, who set the single-season home run record in 2001.**

When Barry Bonds began the 2001 baseball season, he was already recognized as the finest player of his generation. A 10-time All-Star and three-time Most Valuable Player, Bonds was always known as a slugger, but never as *the* slugger. He had never surpassed 50 home runs in a season, and his exceptional all-around skills oddly eliminated his name from the short list of pure power hitters and potential home run kings. When Mark McGwire shattered Roger Maris's single-season home run record in 1998, many observers believed the new record would outlive Maris's. But only three years later, Bonds proved that the sport's best all-around player was also its most powerful.

Bonds homered in his first game of the season, and on April 17, the 36-year-old became only the 17th major leaguer to hit 500 career home runs. He slammed 17 more homers in May and raised his total to 39 by the All-Star break. Opposing pitchers became extremely stingy with strikes, and the media began to shadow his every move, but Bonds remained patient both at the plate and with the press.

Although pitchers continued to pitch around him, Bonds maintained his record home run pace. In the first week of October, he entered a three-game set in Houston with 69 homers, just one shy of McGwire's record. The Astros walked him eight times in 14 plate appearances, but in the ninth inning of the final game of the series, Bonds cracked number 70 off Wilfredo Rodriguez. The following night, in front of the hometown fans at Pacific Bell Park, Bonds hit numbers 71 and 72 off of Dodgers ace Chan Ho Park. Bonds added a 73rd home run in the season's final game to pad his record and ensure himself a fourth MVP award as well as a permanent place in baseball history.

Bonds watched his 73rd home run leave Pac Bell Park on the last day of the 2001 season.

In SI's Words

What makes no apparent sense about this career-best power display is that on July 24 Bonds will turn 37, an age when Mickey Mantle, his closest statistical twin, was finished and most players' best years are well behind them. The average age of the 16 other 500-home run hitters when they belted their career high in homers was 29. Bonds is on track to easily surpass his high of 49—set last season. A dizzying run of 11 homers in 10 games that began on May 17 at Pro Player Stadium against the Florida Marlins and continued through Sunday at Pac Bell Park against the Colorado Rockies had opponents describing Bonds as "the best player I've ever seen" (Atlanta Braves third baseman Chipper Jones), "the best player in the game" (Marlins outfielder Cliff Floyd) and "a guy that you fear as soon as you see him on deck" (Philadelphia Phillies manager Larry Bowa).

–TOM VERDUCCI, JUNE 4, 2001

5

MIAMI'S MAGNIFICENT MAESTRO

In only his second professional season, Dan Marino shattered NFL single-season records for passing yards and touchdown passes.

EPILOGUE

Though Dan Marino could not have known it at the time, his appearance in Super Bowl XIX would be his last. He would go on to produce seasons that rivaled his masterpiece in 1984—including in 1986, when he threw for 44 touchdowns—and he would break every meaningful career passing record in the books. But because Miami never surrounded him with the proper supporting cast, Marino never made it back to the big game during his 17 years in the NFL.

In some seasons the Dolphins' defense was soft, in others Marino's receivers were substandard, and throughout his career the Miami running game was anemic. In his 17 years Marino played with exactly one 1,000-yard rusher. He retired in 2000 as one of the greatest athletes, in any sport, never to have won a title.

Nearly 20 years later, the numbers look like misprints in the year-by-year ledger of the *NFL Record and Fact Book*. Miami Dolphins quarterback Dan Marino finished the 1984 season with 5,084 yards passing and 48 touchdown passes. Needless to say, both of those totals were new NFL records—they work out to an average of 318 yards and three touchdown passes a game—and they remain so today. In 2001, St. Louis Rams quarterback Kurt Warner produced one of the best seasons in recent memory yet still fell 254 yards and 12 touchdown passes short of Marino's outsized totals.

What's more, Marino accomplished the milestones in only his second year in the league, flouting the conventional wisdom that young quarterbacks need roughly four years of seasoning before they are ready for a starting job in the NFL. Dan became the Man in Miami in the sixth game of his rookie season. He led the defending AFC champions to a 7–2 record as a starter, threw 20 touchdown passes and became the first rookie quarterback to be named the starter for the Pro Bowl. So much for seasoning.

And that performance was merely the trailer for the blockbuster Marino delivered in 1984. He threw five touchdown passes in the season opener and never looked back. "The enjoyment of that season," said Dolphins coach Don Shula, "was watching defensive coordinators try from week to week to do something different and have no success." Opponents never could solve Marino and his lightning-quick release, not even San Francisco, which defeated Miami 38–16 in the Super Bowl that season. The 49ers won the game fairly easily, yet they surrendered 318 yards passing to Marino. Just an average day for Dan the Man that year.

Marino was unstoppable against the Steelers in the 1984 AFC Championship, throwing for 421 yards and four touchdowns.

4

A HACK OF A YEAR

> *While the "unbreakable" records of Ruth, Gehrig and Cobb have all been eclipsed, Hack Wilson's mark of 191 RBIs remains supreme.*

One hundred runs batted in in a baseball season has long been the benchmark of an outstanding year for a slugger. One might assume, therefore, that the man who surpassed 100 RBIs before August must have cast an imposing shadow. Imposing? Not really. Odd is more like it. Hack Wilson, a 5' 6", 190-pound centerfielder, sported an 18-inch neck and dainty size 5½ feet. In 1930, Wilson used every sinew in his stout body to swing his way to one of the greatest seasons in baseball history. While producing a .356 batting average for the Chicago Cubs, he pounded 56 homers—a National League record that lasted 68 years—and drove in 191 runs, a record that has never been equaled in the major leagues.

Wilson honed his swing pounding a sledgehammer in a Pennsylvania steel mill before starting his professional baseball career in 1921 with the Martinsburg (W.V.) Blue Sox of the Blue Ridge League. In 1923, John McGraw of the Giants paid $11,000 to bring Wilson to New York. After three undistinguished seasons, however, Wilson was sent to the Cubs, where he blossomed into the National League's most feared power hitter. In 1929 the Cubs reached the World Series, but Wilson missed two fly balls in Game 4, as Chicago lost to the Philadelphia Athletics in five games. Devastated, Wilson began 1930 determined to redeem his gaffes.

Though he started the season slowly, Wilson drove in 73 RBIs by the end of June. After passing the 100 RBI mark on July 28, Wilson embarked on the most torrid stretch of the season, driving in 53 runs in 29 games in August. No one has driven in more runs in a single month in baseball history. He punctuated his record-breaking season by driving in nine runs in the final three games of the season to finish with 191, 21 more than his nearest National League competitor.

EPILOGUE

Just as Hack Wilson was establishing himself as one of the game's brightest stars, his personal battle with alcohol sent his game and his life into a tailspin. He was traded to Brooklyn in 1931 and was completely out of baseball by 1934. His fall from grace dimmed some of the luster that accompanied his glorious 1930 season, and his record was never revered like those of Babe Ruth, whose home run mark of 1927 became the most coveted in baseball. Wilson's record—originally thought to be only 190 RBIs—has proved far more durable. In 1999 a baseball historian discovered an additional, 191st RBI, moving Hack's feat even further out of reach.

Wilson led the National League in home runs four times during his six seasons with the Chicago Cubs.

3

ROYAL REVOLUTIONARY

> *During the 1961–62 season, Oscar Robertson of the Cincinnati Royals became the first and only NBA player to average a "triple-double."*

PROLOGUE

The city of Cincinnati was already familiar with Oscar Robertson's talents when he joined the Royals in 1960. For three years Robertson had starred at the University of Cincinnati, where he had become the NCAA's alltime leading scorer and had led the Bearcats to two consecutive Final Fours. But Robertson's days in college were tainted with the same prejudices he had first experienced as a youth in Indiana. In high school, he had led the all-black Crispus Attucks to two straight Indiana state championships. "I thought then that he was the only high school player I ever saw who could move directly into the pros and immediately be a star," said UCLA's John Wooden. Nevertheless, in-state power Indiana—and UCLA—passed on Robertson. At predominantly white Cincinnati, Robertson endured discrimination at home and when his team traveled. "You were always told what you cannot do," remembered Robertson years later. "All those things I just took in stride and just recently started talking about."

If Oscar Robertson failed to receive proper recognition for averaging a "triple-double" during the 1961–62 season, it is only because the term had yet to be invented. "I was not even aware of it," Robertson later said. Not until Larry Bird and Magic Johnson brought their all-around skills to the NBA in the early 1980s did the expression gain any real significance. Bird and Magic routinely hit double digits in three statistial categories—scoring, rebounding and assists. The Big O averaged 30.8 points, 12.5 rebounds and 11.4 assists a game for an entire season. Not even Bird, Magic or Michael Jordan did that.

The game of basketball took a giant evolutionary step forward when Robertson joined the Cincinnati Royals in 1960. "Oscar just changed the way everything was done," said Sacramento Kings coach Rick Adelman, who faced Robertson as a player. "He was a point guard who could shoot it and pass it. He was so big (6' 5") that he could post up small guys." UCLA coach John Wooden compared Robertson's effortless brilliance to Joe DiMaggio, and Bob Cousy, who coached Robertson in Cincinnati—and held the alltime assists record before Robertson broke it—claimed that the Big O could announce his moves on the court in advance and still be unstoppable.

Robertson's superb triple-double season receives much of the attention in any discussion celebrating his legendary versatility. What's often overlooked, though, and even more impressive, is that Robertson averaged a cumulative triple-double over a five-year span from 1960–65 (30.3 ppg, 10.4 rpg, 10.6 apg). Since Robertson retired in 1974, there have been greater scores, greater playmakers and greater rebounders. But there may never be a greater all-around player.

Robertson's years in Cincinnati were overshadowed by the Celtic dynasty, but he won a title with Milwaukee in 1971.

2

PERFECTION BY
ANY OTHER NAME

> *The 1972 Miami Dolphins etched their*
> *unheralded names in the record book*
> *with the NFL's only perfect season.*

Fueled by an overpowering defense, a steady quarterback and a solid running game, the Chicago Bears were tearing through their 1985 schedule with an eye on history. They had won 12 straight games and seemed destined to complete the NFL's first undefeated regular season since 1972.

Next up on Chicago's schedule were the Miami Dolphins, whose coach, Don Shula, must have appreciated many of the qualities the Bears possessed. For it was Shula who spearheaded that first undefeated season, and his 1972 team also featured superb defense, mistake-free quarterbacking and a buzzsaw running game.

The '72 Dolphins were arguably the greatest football team of all time, with special emphasis on the word "team." Every player subjugated his own ego out of an intense desire to redeem a humiliating 24–3 loss to Dallas in Super Bowl VI. Before that game, Cowboys coach Tom Landry had said that he couldn't name any members of the Dolphins defense. Miami transformed Landry's remark into an enduring nickname, the No-Name Defense, and with linebacker Nick Buoniconti, tackle Manny Fernandez, and safety Dick Anderson leading the way, it held opponents to a league-low 12.2 points per game in '72.

The '72 Dolphins boasted two 1,000-yard rushers, the bruising Larry Csonka and the speedy Mercury Morris. When Bob Griese, the AFC's leading passer in 1971, went down with a broken ankle in the fifth game of the season, 38-year-old veteran Earl Morrall slipped seamlessly into his place.

Yet the Dolphins were two-point underdogs against the Washington Redskins in Super Bowl VII. The game is mostly remembered for Garo Yepremian's comically bungled pass after a botched field goal

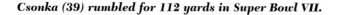

Csonka (39) rumbled for 112 yards in Super Bowl VII.

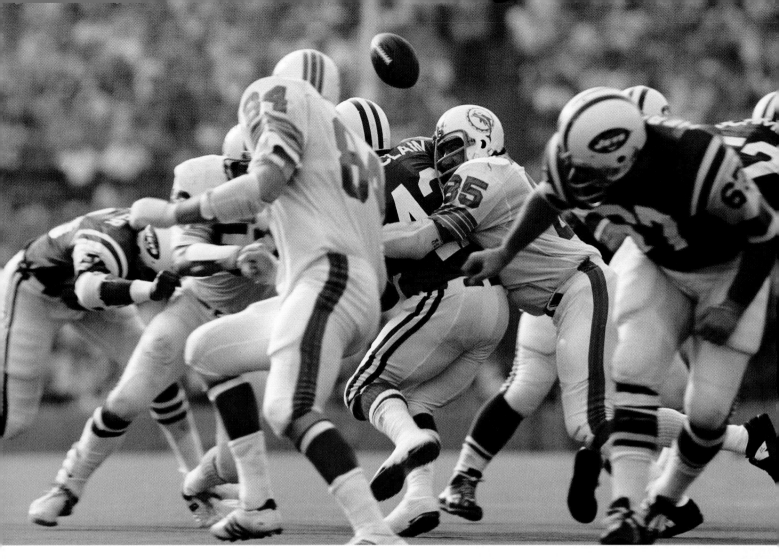

If Buoniconti (above, 85) was the heart of the Dolphins' defense, Griese (opposite, 12) was Shula's cerebral protegé in the offensive huddle. Both players were elected to the Pro Football Hall of Fame.

Shula (right), who would go on to win more games than any coach in NFL history, had already lost two Super Bowls. "If we didn't win [against the Redskins in Supe VII], 16–1 would have been disastrous," he said.

In SI's Words

It was not always easy, and far less dramatic than it might have been, but the Miami Dolphins finally demonstrated rather conclusively that they are the biggest fish in the pro football pond. In the seventh Super Bowl they defeated the Washington Redskins 14–7 before 81,706 sweltering and smog-beset fans in the Los Angeles Memorial Coliseum. This meant that the Dolphins went an entire season without a loss, 17 straight. No other NFL team has ever gone undefeated for a season, and no other club is likely to do it again soon, either. On the record, then, Miami is the best club in pro football history.

The Dolphins won the game with a nearly impeccable first half; with an extraordinarily accurate passer in quarterback Bob Griese; with a rhino of a runner, Larry Csonka; and, above all, with a defense that may have been No Names, but was plenty of adjectives. Try tough, tight, dashing and daring for starters.

—*TEX MAULE, JANUARY 22, 1973*

attempt in the fourth quarter, but it was equally notable for providing Miami its definitive stamp on the season and NFL history. While Griese, back from his injury, drove the offense with methodical efficiency, the No-Name Defense stymied Washington at every turn. They intercepted quarterback Billy Kilmer three times and held a 14–0 lead in the fourth quarter. When Yepremian's gaffe opened the door for the Skins, the No-Name Defense slammed it shut again, preserving Miami's 14–7 triumph and its record season.

The mark went unchallenged until the '85 Bears, so it was poetic justice that Shula's Dolphins defeated Chicago 38–24 on that Monday night. Shula's team, which made it look easy in '72, proved how difficult it is to run the table in the NFL. As Miami running back Jim Kiick said, "At the time, it wasn't considered that big of an achievement. But every year that passes, it's more unbelievable. I don't think it will ever be done again."

THE GAME THAT RUTH BUILT

In his first season with the New York Yankees, Babe Ruth hit more home runs than any team in the American League.

Babe Ruth was walking mythology, a juggernaut on and off the field, an American icon. His celebrated numbers remain a statistical freight train that still chugs through the heartland of the national pastime: 714 home runs—60 of them in one season—2,213 runs batted in and a career average of .342. But the Babe's first year with the New York Yankees was arguably his most Ruthian. In 1920, Ruth clubbed 54 homers, ushering in an exciting era of offense that made baseball America's game.

Pre-Ruth baseball was a very different sport from the one we know today. Runs were scarce, and the offensive weapons of the age were the bunt and the stolen base. Ruth changed everything: "I swing big, with everything I've got," he said. "I hit big or I miss big." Watching him whiff was almost as exciting as watching him connect. When Ruth hit 29 home runs for the Boston Red Sox in 1919—his team-mates combined for only four—he established a new single-season record. But Boston's owner, Broadway showman Harry Frazee, needed cash and decided to sell his 24-year old superstar to the New York Yankees.

A pulled rib muscle limited Ruth during the first weeks of the 1920 season and it wasn't until May 1—and four straight losses to the "Ruth-less" Red Sox—that New York's prized purchase crushed one over the roof of the Polo Grounds. Finally healthy, he hammered 11 more homers before the month was out, and another dozen in June. On July 15, Ruth matched his single-season record with his 29th

Ruth hit 54 of New York's 115 home runs in 1920; no other team in the league hit more than 50.

In SI's Words

There the batter was, looking bigger than the House itself, larger even than his myth: moonfaced and broad-backed and shaped like an inverted eggplant, dragging his bat toward the plate. No man on earth had more nicknames than George Herman Ruth. The Babe. The Man. The Bambino. The Home Run King. The Circuit Smasher. Herman the Great. Homeric Herman. The Bulky Monarch. The King of Clout. His Eminence. The Sultan of Swat. . . .

[Nearly 70] years have passed since he made his last appearance as a player, in a Boston Braves uniform, yet he remains the purest original ever to have played big league base-ball. For all that he did in his 22 sea-sons in the majors, surely nothing left a deeper imprint on the game than the force and flair he brought to bear in striking the ball.

—*WILLIAM NACK, AUGUST 24, 1998*

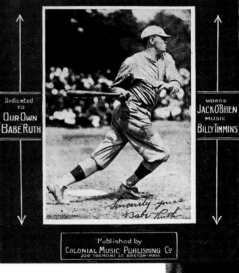

home run, but Ruth was far from finished. Despite missing 12 games during the 154-game season, Ruth finished with 54 home runs, more than any team in the American League. St. Louis's George Sisler finished second to the Babe—with 19.

The Yankees finished in third place, three games behind the pennant-winning Cleveland Indians, but the season was a roaring success. Attendance at the Polo Grounds paralleled the Babe's achievements, and the Yankees became the first organization to surpass one million fans for a season. Three years later, the Yankees would move into a cavernous new home in the Bronx to accommodate the throngs of new fans, and the Yankees began a dynasty that has never been matched in American professional sports.

Ruth's skill at the plate inspired songs (inset) and won him new fans (right) wherever he went.

LEGENDARY STREAKS

INTRODUCTION

It doesn't matter if it lasts for minutes, days, months or years. It can be a string of field goals in a single game, a spell of victories that endures for the better part of a season, or a run of championships spanning years. Whatever form it takes, a streak is as delicate as a hothouse flower. One bad bounce, a shot that rims out, or an outstanding defensive play—not to mention an off night, an injury, or a lapse in concentration— and a hot streak can be extinguished.

Streaks are the most tenuous, and mysterious, elements in sports. Athletes frequently speak of being "in the zone," a quasi-mystical state wherein they can do no wrong. Every shot falls, every pass is on the money and every hit is—to paraphrase Willie Keeler, owner of one of baseball's famous streaks—where they ain't. No one has been able to isolate what brings this condition on, and few have been able to control how long it lasts; athletes simply ride it, like a wave, and try to get the most out of a hot spell before it subsides.

One way of looking at a streak, then, is as the fabled "zone," extended indefinitely. Much of the thrill of witnessing an athlete or team on a roll lies in the Hitchcockian suspense of it all: When will it end? "Will DiMaggio get another hit?" baseball fans were asking all summer in 1941. "Will the Lakers win yet another game?" wondered NBA fans in 1971–72, as Los Angeles reeled off 33 victories in a row. As we've said, at any moment and for a litany of reasons, the answer could have been no. Streaks are ascents into increasingly rarefied air.

But as fragile as they are in the making, streaks often prove quite durable once fired in history's kiln. Most of the ones you'll read about in the following pages have lasted for decades. Some may never be eclipsed. When we sat down to rank them, three feats rose above the pack: the Boston

The professionalism of Ripken (opposite), the competitiveness of Bill Russell (left) and the focus of Woods (above) fueled their respective streaks.

Celtics' stupefying run of NBA titles from 1959 to '66; DiMaggio's epic 56-game hitting streak in 1941—the ultimate streak; and Tiger Woods's recent sweep of the PGA majors. These, like all streaks, certainly involved luck and persistence, but they are primarily about sheer talent and utter dominance, the likes of which we may never see again.

After we set DiMaggio, the Celtics and Woods aside, though, the waters of comparison muddied considerably. Take Cal Ripken Jr.'s 16-year streak of 2,632 consecutive games played. While undeniably impressive, it may have more to do with endurance and good health than surpassing skill. On the other hand, no one is likely to threaten Ripken's record in our lifetime, and further, there was an astounding six-year span during the streak in which Ripken played every inning of every game for the Orioles. Hence, Ripken goes in at No. 6— in the middle of our pack of extraordinary streaks.

There are feats in this chapter that many fans will remember, such as cancer survivor Lance Armstrong's string of Tour de France victories, and some that may not be so familiar, such as Johnny Unitas's streak of throwing at least one touchdown pass in 47 straight games. We're happy to shine the spotlight on that hidden gem, which was accomplished from 1956 to '60, when NFL teams were not nearly as keen on the forward pass as they are now.

Unitas's streak remains an NFL record, and of all the legendary passers who've followed Johnny U, not one has come close to it. Dan Marino is second on that list, with a string of 30 games. Which points up the unique, almost arcane, nature of streaks. A mysterious alchemy of conditions—skill, consistency and good fortune—must prevail for streaks to grow. And charting their progress is one of sports' most dramatic and enduring fascinations.

15

TOUR DE FORCE

> *After beating cancer, Lance Armstrong whipped his cycling peers in three straight Tours de France.*

Lance Armstrong would be the first to tell you that cycling is a team sport. He's right, of course, but that takes nothing from the staggering individual requirements of cycling's premier event, the Tour de France. Riders traverse more than 2,000 miles in only three weeks, and though they may draft off of teammates occasionally, they are mostly powered by two wheels, two legs and two lungs. It's one of the most grueling events in sports.

So imagine attempting it less than three years after being diagnosed with advanced testicular cancer and being given a coin-toss chance of making it to your 26th birthday. Like his teammates on the Tour, Armstrong's friends and loved ones could do only so much to help him through cancer surgery and three months of chemotherapy in 1996.

Thirty-three months after having tumors removed from his lungs and brain, Armstrong not only attempted the Tour but dominated it, winning by more than seven minutes. The battle with cancer had left him 15 pounds lighter, and with his newfound sleekness, he developed an indefatigable climbing ability in the mountain stages. He iced his first Tour victory with an astonishing ride on the first day in the Alps.

In 2000 he was more cautious, biding his time in 16th place before making his move in the Pyrenees to claim a second Tour. The following year he was downright cagey, playing possum in 23rd place before rocketing up a 12-mile ascent on l'Alpe d'Huez, leaving world-class cyclists in his wake. He became the first U.S. rider to win three straight Tours.

"It's been a long time since cycling had a real boss," said Johan Bruyneel, a former rider and the director of Armstrong's U.S. Postal Service team. "Right now in the Tour de France, people consider Lance the boss." For his part, Armstrong says, "I'm a cancer survivor first and a cyclist second." And an inspiration on both counts.

In SI's Words

When you are Lance Armstrong and you've survived 12 tumors on your lungs, two on your brain and a cancer-ravaged testicle the size of a lemon, the French Alps start to look like speed bumps. . . .

So no wonder Armstrong delivered two of the most remarkable days in Tour de France history last week, tearing through the French Alps as if he were double-parked somewhere, dancing on his pedals, nobody coming within a yodel of him. . . . Unless the Eiffel Tower falls on him, Armstrong will become the fifth man to win the Tour de France three years in a row. "It's just so much fun," he said. Unless you're trying to catch him. "We keep waiting for this man to have a bad day," said the director of rival Team Telekom, Rudy Pevenage, "but the only bad day he has is the day after celebrating in Paris."

—*RICK REILLY, JULY 30, 2001*

Armstrong finished fourth in the 15th stage of the 2000 Tour, adding 2:31 to his overall lead on the pack.

14

GOLDEN GOODBYE

With his final leap at the 1996 Atlanta Games, Carl Lewis won his fourth consecutive Olympic gold medal in the long jump.

In SI's Words

It wasn't supposed to happen. It couldn't have happened. But the man who made the U.S Olympic team by a mere inch, the man who made it to the finals only by grabbing onto the last handrail on the last caboose, the oldest man in the field won the gold with ancient legs, gray hair and a heart that stays forever young.

Carl Lewis beat age, gravity, history, logic and the world on Monday night at a rocking Olympic Stadium in Atlanta to win the gold medal in the long jump . . .

You try to give the man a gold watch, and he steals your gold medal instead. You ask him to pass the torch, and he sets your Olympics on fire instead. . . .

When they called him forward to his last Olympic victory stand in that sweet Georgia night, he covered his face with his hands again and again, as if even he couldn't believe this. And before they played the first note, he was crying again.

—*RICK REILLY, AUGUST 5, 1996*

It might very well have been the most satisfying moment of Carl Lewis's career, which is saying something. This is the man who equaled Jesse Owens's landmark feat of winning four track and field gold medals in a single Olympics. This is the man whose trophy case contained nine Olympic medals, eight of them gold.

Lewis was accustomed to multiple-medal hauls at the Games, but on a soft summer night in Atlanta in 1996, one gold medal would do just fine. At age 35, Lewis capped his magnificent career by winning the long jump for his fourth consecutive Olympic victory in the event. He joined discus thrower Al Oerter as the only men to win four Olympic gold medals in a single discipline.

And it very nearly didn't happen. At the U.S. Olympic trials, Lewis qualified for the long jump by exactly one inch. He missed the cut in every other event. Once in Atlanta, though, Lewis made the most of what he knew would be his last chance on the Olympic stage. He leaped 27' 10¾" and won the gold medal by 8¼ inches over James Beckford of Jamaica. It was the ninth gold of his career, placing him second on the alltime list of Olympic athletes with the most gold medals.

"You've just seen a great performer at the end of his career," said Lewis's coach, Tom Tellez. "People thought he couldn't do it, but he did. He's the greatest athlete I've ever seen."

Lewis jumped 28' 7½"—the longest leap of his Olympic career—to win gold at the 1988 Games in Seoul.

13

SOONER SUPREMACY

> **Coach Bud Wilkinson led Oklahoma to two national championships during a five-year stretch in which his teams won 47 straight games.**

Coach Bud Wilkinson came to Oklahoma at a time when the state and the university were eager to dispel the Okie stigma created during the dust bowl years of the 1930s. Wilkinson, who became the Sooners head coach in 1947, turned out to be exactly what the beleaguered Oklahomans needed. He transformed Oklahoma's football team into a national powerhouse, winning 14 conference titles and three national championships before he retired in 1963. In the mid-1950s the Sooners were as unbeatable as any team has ever been, winning a record 47 games in a row.

Two weeks after a 28–21 season-opening loss to Notre Dame in 1953, Oklahoma beat Texas 19–14 to begin the longest winning streak in Division I college football history. Seven victories later, the Sooners upset undefeated Maryland 7–0 in the Orange Bowl.

In 1954 Oklahoma outscored its opponents 304–62, including a 65–0 blowout against rival Kansas. The next year, Oklahoma shut out five opponents, led the nation in scoring and won the national championship. In 1956 Oklahoma hammered Texas 45–0, pounded Notre Dame 40–0 and broke Washington's record of 39 straight victories by extending its winning streak to 40 games. Colorado was the only team to come within 20 points of the Sooners during their second consecutive national championship season.

By 1957, the core of Oklahoma's championship teams had graduated, but they were still one of the strongest teams in the country. They won their first seven games and entered their Nov. 16 matchup against Notre Dame as 18-point favorites. The Fighting Irish, however, ended the Sooners' winning streak with a 7–0 upset. As the gloomy Oklahoma fans filed out of the stadium, the announcer offered solace. "Come back next Saturday, folks. That's when a new winning streak starts."

CLOSE CALL

During a November 1956 game at Colorado, the streak appeared to be in jeopardy as the Sooners trailed 19–6 at halftime. Coach Wilkinson burst into the locker room and lectured his team. He told his reeling players that they were unworthy to wear Oklahoma uniforms and ordered them to take off their jerseys. Stunned, the Sooners complied. They stripped off their shirts and sat in the cold as their coach stormed out of the room. Just before the second half began, Wilkinson returned with a different attitude. "Nobody in this stadium believes you can win this game," he said. "Except me."

Rejuvenated by Wilkinson's words, the Sooners pulled their jerseys back on and stopped the Buffaloes cold in the second half. The Sooners came back to win 27–19, and the streak continued well into the next season.

Wilkinson (far right) established a winning tradition at Oklahoma, going 145-29-4 during his 17 years with the Sooners.

12

L.A. STORY

> **Wilt, West and the rest of the Los Angeles Lakers won 33 games in a row on their way to a 69–13 record and the 1972 NBA title.**

THE STOPPER

As if to say, "Okay, you broke our record, that's enough," the defending champion Milwaukee Bucks ended the Lakers' historic winning streak at 33 games, defeating them 120–104 in Milwaukee on Jan. 9, 1972. A year earlier, with second-year center Lew Alcindor leading the way, the Bucks had won 20 in a row to establish the milestone that the Lakers would obliterate.

In 1971, Alcindor changed his name to Kareem Abdul-Jabbar, but everything else about the Bucks remained the same. They won 63 games, Abdul-Jabbar led the league in scoring, and two months after they ended the record winning streak, the Bucks nearly derailed the Laker express again in the Western Conference finals. Milwaukee won the first game in a rout and pushed the series to a sixth game. The Lakers squeaked by in that one, 104–100, to dethrone the Bucks and move on to the Finals.

The Los Angeles Lakers had barreled like a runaway train through the Milwaukee Bucks' NBA record for consecutive victories (20) in 1971, and they showed no signs of slowing down. As they closed in on 30 straight wins, center Wilt Chamberlain joked that the team's remarkable run reminded him of his pre-NBA stint with the Harlem Globetrotters. Wilt and the Trotters had "won" 445 games in a row.

Of course the Lakers' NBA opponents were a far cry from the Washington Generals, but they did have something in common with the Globetrotters' perennial foils. As Los Angeles forward Jim McMillian said, "During the streak we knew before we walked out onto the court that we were going to win. And the other team knew it, too."

Their confidence was born of a new system and a new attitude, both of which were instilled by a new coach, Bill Sharman. Sharman asked guard Jerry West, a superb scorer, to pass more, and West led the league in assists. He asked Chamberlain to focus on rebounding and defense, and Chamberlain topped the league with 19.2 rebounds a game. With the superstars shining selflessly, the rest of the cast flourished—and it seemed the Lakers couldn't lose.

Los Angeles eventually won 33 games in a row, a record for professional sports. They would finish at 69–13—the best record in league history at the time—but all of it would have been reduced to trivia-quiz fodder had the Lakers not won the NBA title. After dropping the first game of the Finals to New York, they reeled off another streak: four straight to cap a near perfect season.

> **Without injured center Willis Reed, the Knicks were powerless to stop Chamberlain (13) during the 1972 Finals.**

11

QUEEN OF THE COURT

Martina Navratilova won 74 consecutive matches in 1984, the zenith of a four-year stretch in which she dominated women's tennis.

On Jan. 15, 1984, Hana Mandlikova upset Martina Navratilova in the finals of the Virginia Slims of California, ending Navratilova's 54-match winning streak two shy of Chris Evert's alltime record. Navratilova had just completed the most dominating season in tennis history—going 86–1 and winning three Grand Slam tournaments—and the loss to the younger player may have suggested a letdown. Instead, the loss seemed to motivate Navratilova, who rebounded to obliterate Evert's record by winning her next 74 matches.

Navratilova's dedication to strength training and conditioning set the standard for female athletes, and her serve-and-volley strategy revolutionized a sport long dominated by baseliners. Her mental approach to the game was equally focused. "She won the matches before I stepped on the court," said Evert. "I knew I couldn't win. Mentally, she had already won. And I was No. 2 in the world . . . Imagine what she was doing to the other players. She was invincible."

The rest of the tour was equally frustrated. Pam Shriver at least shared some of Navratilova's glory, partnering with her to win 109 straight doubles matches from 1983 to '85. "The only way of stopping her is to drive over her feet in the car park," said Shriver's coach, Don Candy.

Navratilova won 13 straight tournaments during her singles streak, including the season's first three majors. By the time she reached the semifinals of the Australian Open, in December 1984, Navratilova had gone 128–1 in the previous 18 months and was only two victories away from tennis's first Grand Slam since 1970. Helena Sukova, a 19-year-old from Czechoslovakia, ended Navratilova's streak in a thrilling three-set semifinal in which Navratilova staved off five match points before succumbing. With the streak finally over, perhaps Navratilova was now due for that inevitable letdown. No such luck for her unfortunate competition: In 1985 she went 84–5.

In SI's Words

Like only a very few athletes before her at the peak of their powers—Bobby Jones, Babe Ruth, Edwin Moses—Navratilova is simply too good for her sport. As she herself put it, not unbecomingly, "I have transcended another level." And nobody is following. Chris Evert is royalty in retreat. In the French Open singles final in June 1984, Navratilova routed her 6–3, 6–1 to extend her winning streak against Evert to 11 matches. Hana Mandlikova and Kathy Horvath, the only ones to beat Navratilova in the past 12 months, are comparative children who happened to have one charmed day. She avenged both of those losses in Paris.
—CURRY KIRKPATRICK, JUNE 18, 1984

From 1982 to '86, Navratilova went 428–14 and won 13 Grand Slams, including Wimbledon in 1983.

ALEXANDER THE GREAT

> *Alexander Karelin of Russia ruled Greco-Roman wrestling with an iron fist during his 13-year winning streak.*

"Everything I do not get with my physical ability," said imposing Russian wrestler Alexander Karelin, "I get with my reputation." Standing 6' 3" and weighing 290 pounds, Karelin terrorized his competition in the superheavyweight division of Greco-Roman wrestling for 13 straight years. During that span, no one beat him, and most were just happy to escape the mat in one piece.

Born and raised in the harsh climate of Siberia, Karelin caught the world's attention as a 21-year-old by winning Olympic gold at the 1988 Games in Seoul. Of his five opponents, only Rangel Gerovsky of Bulgaria lasted the full six minutes with Karelin, and Gerovsky paid the price by falling victim to the Russian's patented reverse body lift. Many of Karelin's future opponents would simply submit rather than allow themselves to be lifted by their hips and slammed onto their backs. Perhaps 1984 gold medalist Jeff Blatnick put it best, describing what he felt in the clutches of Karelin's reverse lift: "Every hair on the back of my neck raised up. I was scared. Intense fear."

Karelin was unstoppable, breezing through European and world championships alike. Entering the 1992 Olympics in Barcelona, Karelin had not been defeated since the 1987 Soviet Nationals. He dispatched four of his five Olympic competitors in a total of 5 minutes and 32 seconds, en route to his second gold. At the Atlanta Games in '96 he struck gold again by outlasting American Matt Ghaffari 1–0 in the final. Karelin reached the gold-medal match at the 2000 Games in Sydney, as well, and when he stepped onto the mat to face Rulon Gardner of the U.S., he had not surrendered a single point in 10 years. Which made Gardner's 1–0 upset all the more remarkable.

"Wrestling him," said Ghaffari (bottom, during the 1990 Grand Masters), "is like wrestling King Kong."

THE STOPPER

Alexander Karelin was a Russian hero and a virtual lock for a fourth consecutive gold medal at the 2000 Olympics. Few observers gave Rulon Gardner any chance against the nine-time world champion. Gardner had faced Karelin once before: In 1997 he had been reverse-lifted three times in a 5–0 drubbing. Nevertheless, Gardner advanced to the final and, unbelievably, scored a point on Karelin in the second period to take a 1–0 lead. The score remained that way at the end of the third period, and the match moved into overtime because neither had scored at least three points.

In overtime, Gardner resisted all of Karelin's attempts to score, and the referee declared Gardner the winner. The streak had ended, and Karelin ascended to the second step of the medals podium—as one Russian newspaper put it—"as to a gallows."

9

SWEET AS SUGAR

> *The sweet science never knew a greater warrior than Sugar Ray Robinson, who went unbeaten in 91 fights spanning eight years.*

To hardcore boxing aficionados, there is only one Sugar Ray. Sugar Ray Robinson—born Walker Smith—was synonymous with boxing greatness. His speed, power and impressive style earned him his nickname, and his reign during boxing's golden age places him at the top of any list of the best pound-for-pound boxers of all time. In his prime, he could outpunch, outsmart or outbox any opponent, and from 1943 to '51, he didn't lose a single bout.

Robinson won his first 40 professional bouts before facing Jake LaMotta in February 1943. Robinson had beaten LaMotta before, but the Bronx Bull, as LaMotta was nicknamed, handed Robinson the first loss of his career. Robinson revenged the setback just three weeks later, and he did not lose again for eight years and 91 fights.

Fighting as much as 19 times a year, Robinson remained in supreme condition. In 1946 Robinson got up off the canvas to defeat Tommy Bell and win the welterweight title. He defended his title five times and fought many non-championship bouts between 1946 and 1950. After dispatching all the willing welterweights, Robinson challenged LaMotta for the world middleweight title on Feb. 14, 1951. In the sixth and final showdown of a great rivalry, Robinson stopped LaMotta in the 13th round for the title.

Five months later in London, Englishman Randy Turpin upset Robinson and took his middleweight title. It was Robinson's first loss since 1943, but he quickly made amends. Two months later, he knocked out Turpin in New York to recapture his crown. Robinson lost and regained the middleweight title three more times before he finally retired in 1965, and he was never the fighter as a middleweight that he had been as a welterweight. But as *SI* wrote in 1957, "He is, in truth, a lion among champions. His feats are unequaled in ring history."

In SI's Words

It is eerie, the similarity in technique between the three of them—first Robinson, then Ali, now Leonard. It was Robinson who was the original, the handsome master boxer with matchless hand speed, charisma and the fine legs of a figure skater. It was Robinson who went 123-1-2 to begin his career and become the welterweight champion, and it was Robinson who then went on to win the middleweight title those incredible five times. . . . He won the national Golden Gloves featherweight title in 1939 at age 17, when Joe Louis was champion of the world. He lost his final fight at 44, to the No. 1 middleweight contender, Joey Archer, in 1965, when Ali was champ. In the years from 1945 to the middle of 1951 Robinson, at 147 pounds, was unbeatable and irresistible. To the men of that era, and to some of their many sons and daughters, Leonard can only be a Sugar substitute.
—RALPH WILEY, JULY 13, 1987

Robinson lost the middleweight title to Gene Fullmer in January 1957 but regained it with a fifth-round KO in May.

8

LORD OF THE LINKS

> *Every great golf season pales in comparison to the year Byron Nelson had in 1945, when he won 11 straight tournaments.*

CLOSE CALL

With an average margin of victory of 6.25 strokes in the 16 stroke-play events he won that season, Byron Nelson had very few close calls in 1945. But he received a scare at the Victory National Open, in Chicago in late June, while vying for his eighth consecutive victory.

Nelson wrenched his back during a long-drive contest before the main event, and the pain was enough to make him consider withdrawing from the tournament. After a tee-time decision to play, Nelson took the lead, which he held by one stroke over his good friend Harold (Jug) McSpaden as the tournament entered its final round.

McSpaden began Sunday with a birdie, but Nelson trumped him with an eagle. On the third hole McSpaden made a triple bogey to Nelson's par, and Lord Byron never looked back, pulling away for a seven-stroke victory. That's what qualified as a close call in Nelson's extraordinary year.

Even with Tiger Woods prowling PGA courses, it's difficult to imagine any golfer approaching Byron Nelson's 11-tournament winning streak of 1945. In the 57 years since, no golfer has come within four of his streak. Woods won six in a row in 1999–2000, equaling Ben Hogan's run of 1948. Both men were the best of their age, and both fell far short of Nelson's achievement.

Critics point out that Nelson achieved his dominance against a field depleted by World War II. But they often forget that the two other top players of the era, Hogan and Sam Snead, returned from serving their country in time to play 18 and 26 events, respectively, that season. Hogan ranks with the greatest golfers of all time, and Snead is the PGA's alltime leader in victories.

Regardless of the level of competition, Nelson's play in 1945 was nothing short of astounding. He shot 19 consecutive rounds under 70 and finished the season with 18 victories. Most of his wins were stamped with exclamation points: Nelson averaged a score of 67.68 in final rounds during his historic streak.

A genteel Texan whose parents named him after the poet Lord Byron, Nelson said that he played golf to make enough money to fulfill his lifelong dream of owning a ranch. That dream inched closer to reality in 1944, when Nelson won 10 tournaments. After his season for the ages in '45, it became a reality. Nelson retired to his North Texas spread the following season, at 34, his place in golf's pantheon secure.

In the 30 tournaments Nelson entered in 1945, he won 18 and finished second seven times.

COLT .47

> *It's one of the most enduring yet least appreciated NFL records: From 1956 to '60 Johnny Unitas threw a touchdown pass in 47 straight games.*

"The most important thing of all about Unitas," said Colts' coach Weeb Ewbank, "is that he had a real hunger. This was a kid who wanted success and didn't have it so long that he wasn't about to waste it when it came." By the time Johnny Unitas won the starting quarterback job for the Baltimore Colts in 1957, he had been ignored by big-time colleges, cut by the Pittsburgh Steelers, and exiled to semi-pro ball in the sandlots of western Pennsylvania. Unitas fed off the adversity, and when he finally got his chance, he took advantage. From 1956 to '60, the man with the flattop haircut and hightop shoes threw touchdown passes in 47 consecutive games, a record that has never been seriously challenged.

Unitas was forced into action when Baltimore's quarterback George Shaw broke his leg in 1956. The Colts finished only 5–7 that season, but Unitas tossed touchdown passes in each of the final three games to begin his streak. The following year, Unitas threw touchdown passes in all 12 games and was named the league's MVP, as the Colts finished 7–5. But it was in 1958 that Unitas established himself as a legend. He completed a league-high 19 touchdown passes and led Baltimore to the NFL title game, a classic 23–17 overtime win against New York.

In 1959 Unitas set a league record with 32 TD passes, and the Colts won their second straight NFL championship. His streak ran through the 10th game of the 1960 season before it ended—at 47 games—against the Los Angeles Rams, the team it had started against. Unitas threw 102 touchdowns during his remarkable run, and the Colts became the top team in the NFL.

In the four decades since, the NFL has become a more pass-oriented league, yet Dan Marino's 30-game stretch in the mid-'80s is the closest anyone has come to Unitas's record. Like his signature look, perhaps Johnny U's streak is one of a kind.

Unitas led the Colts to an overtime victory in the 1958 NFL title game—commonly called the greatest game of all time.

In SI's Words

The Baltimore Colts, ticking off the yards with sure strength under the magnificent direction of quarterback Johnny Unitas, scored the touchdown which brought sudden death to New York and the first championship to hungry Baltimore. . . .

The Colts won because they are a superbly well-armed football team. They spent the first half picking at the small flaws in the Giants defense, doing it surely and competently under the guidance of Unitas. . . .

Unitas, a tall, thin man who looks a little stooped in his uniform, took his time throwing, and when he threw, the passes were flat and hard as a frozen rope, and on target. He varied the Baltimore attack from time to time by sending Alan Ameche thumping into the Giants line.

The Giants defense, unable to overpower the Colts as it had the Browns, shifted and changed and tried tricks, and Unitas, more often than not, switched his signal at the last possible second to take advantage of Giants weakness.

—TEX MAULE, JANUARY 5, 1959

6

DEATH. TAXES. CAL RIPKEN JR.

Foremost among Cal Ripken Jr.'s many contributions to baseball is his monumental record of 2,632 consecutive games played.

CLOSE CALL

In the spring of 1995, when he was only 121 games shy of Lou Gehrig's record, Cal Ripken Jr.'s streak almost came to an unfortunate halt. It wasn't an inside fastball or twisted ankle that threatened to end the chase but the players' strike that canceled the 1994 World Series and spilled over into the '95 season.

Off-season negotiations had reached an impasse, and team owners planned on beginning the new season with replacement players. Although the players' union seemed willing to make one high-profile exception if the owners went through with their plan, Ripken refused to cross the picket line to extend the streak. Baltimore's owner, Peter Angelos, a former union lawyer, made sure that Ripken would never have to make that decision. He incensed his fellow owners by refusing to field a team of replacement players. Period.

On Opening Day, the owners and players finally agreed to play the 1995 season, and Ripken's victory lap later that summer helped heal baseball's wounds. "I'm not sure how I would have reacted if the streak ended," Ripken said. "But I'm glad I'll never have to find out."

On Sept. 20, 1998, Albert Belle of the Chicago White Sox became baseball's active leader for consecutive games played with 325. The real event of the day, however, took place in Baltimore's Camden Yards, where the Orioles' Cal Ripken Jr. was honored for doing nothing at all. When the Orioles took the field against the New York Yankees—whose Lou Gehrig set the iron-man standard—Ripken was not in the lineup for the first time since May 1982, and the Streak finally ended after three presidents, eight managers and 2,632 games.

"He is the Streak," said ex-teammate Rafael Palmeiro, "and the Streak is him." For 16 years, Ripken went to work every day, and for 16 years, his manager penciled his name in the lineup. In a sport where injuries range from the severe (broken leg) to the silly (punctured eardrum from a Q-tip—Look it up!), Ripken once played in 8,243 straight innings, a number even more impressive considering that he played shortstop, the second-most grueling position in baseball. He played with a twisted ankle, with an aching back and with a broken nose. When he finally eclipsed Gehrig's "unbreakable" record of 2,130 games on Sept. 6, 1995, he not only made history but also revitalized interest in a sport on the brink of self-destruction.

Palmeiro's words reveal a hidden truth: The Streak often overshadowed the man. If Ripken had never broken Gehrig's record, he still would be a Hall-of-Fame talent. He won two American League MVP awards, retired with 3,184 hits, won two Gold Gloves for defense and hit more home runs than any other shortstop in history. Moreover, at 6' 4", 220 pounds, Ripken proved that a big man could handle the defensive demands of shortstop while contributing at the plate as well. "He set the standard," said 6' 3" Derek Jeter. "Shortstops were short, defensive. Now the position is offensive as well. He set the tone for the rest of us."

Ripken kept going for three more years after he broke Gehrig's record at Camden Yards on Sept. 6, 1995.

5

HOLY MOSES!

> **Edwin Moses went 10 years without losing a 400-meter hurdles race, a streak encompassing four world records and 122 victories.**

"Nobody can walk on a track and beat me unless they have an extraordinary day and I have a bad day," said hurdler Edwin Moses in 1985. Moses didn't have a bad day for nearly 10 years, winning 122 consecutive 400-meter hurdle races, the longest winning streak in track history.

Moses burst upon the track scene in 1976 to win the Olympic gold medal in Montreal. It was only his fifth international race after running for little-known Morehouse College in Georgia. But Moses' ideal build, ferocious drive and rhythmic form made up for any lack of racing pedigree. His unusually long legs enabled him to take fewer strides between hurdles than other hurdlers. "Edwin's advantage is that the other fellas actually have to jump over the hurdles," his ex-wife, Myrella Moses, said in 1984, explaining Moses' ability to glide effortlessly around the track.

On Aug. 26, 1977, Harald Schmid of West Germany beat Moses in Berlin. Almost a decade would pass before Moses would lose again. He missed out on a chance to repeat as Olympic champion when the United States boycotted the 1980 Moscow Games, but he continued to dominate, breaking the world record four times. When he won Olympic gold again in Los Angeles in 1984, the streak had reached 109 races, and Moses had produced the most dominant career in track history. "He can be at 75, 80 percent and still beat everyone else," said Dr. Leroy Walker, the U.S Olympic coach in 1976.

When the streak finally came to an end on June 4, 1987, in Madrid, Moses owned 17 of the 20 best times ever recorded in the 400 hurdles. He recovered from the loss to win a bronze medal at the 1988 Olympics in Seoul, and although the competition had finally chased him down, his greatness has never been equaled.

Moses finished first—where else?—in Koblenz, Germany, in 1983, clocking 47.02, a world record that stood for nine years.

WESTWOOD WIZARDRY

The UCLA basketball team reeled off 88 consecutive victories from 1971 to '74, capping an era in which it won nine titles in 10 years.

Vince Lombardi once said, "Winning isn't a sometimes thing, it's an all-the-time thing." No coach epitomized that maxim more than UCLA's John Wooden. The Wizard of Westwood led the Bruins to 10 national championships, including seven in a row, while maintaining a dignity and a reverence for the game that rivaled his success. His teams measured themselves not only against their opponents, but also against perfection. For 88 games from 1971 to '74, UCLA was just that: perfect.

After an 89–82 loss to Notre Dame in January 1971, UCLA forward Sidney Wicks was inconsolable. He told Wooden, "I just can't believe we lost."

"Then I suggest not to do it again," replied Wooden.

It was not quite as simple as that, but the Bruins swept the rest of their games and won their fifth straight NCAA title with a 68–62 win over Villanova. Despite graduating four starters, UCLA was even better the next year. Sophomore center Bill Walton—who had dominated the 1971 NCAA champs in practice as a member of the freshman team—joined the squad and led them to a perfect 30–0 season. The team's 81–76 defeat of Florida State in the NCAA final, however, was not up to UCLA's high standards—at least in the eyes of its star. "One of the things that coach Wooden was so great at teaching was that your sense of competition was not so much based on beating the opposition,

With Walton at center, the Bruins produced back-to-back undefeated seasons and won two NCAA titles.

THE STOPPER

Notre Dame was ranked No. 2 in the country, but they were heavy underdogs against UCLA on Jan. 19, 1974. The Bruins had won 88 games in a row and had creamed the Irish by 19 points the year before. But head coach Digger Phelps had studied UCLA's tendencies and John Wooden's habits and felt good about his team's chances.

Trailing by 11 with 3:30 to go, Phelps made an adjustment to his full-court press, and UCLA turned the ball over five straight times. Wooden, who frowned upon calling timeouts, didn't stop the clock to regroup until Notre Dame had gone ahead, 71–70, with 29 seconds remaining. The Bruins had the last chance but took five desperate shots that caromed off the rim as the clock expired.

but playing and beating an ideal opponent of great quality and to play well yourself," Walton said. "I just don't feel that we had a good game, and myself in particular."

Walton and the Bruins had an opportunity to "redeem" themselves in 1973. UCLA went undefeated for the second consecutive season, breaking San Francisco's NCAA-record 60-game winning streak. In the NCAA final against Memphis State, Walton scored 44 points and missed only one shot as the Bruins won 87–66.

All good things must come to an end, and in UCLA's case, the streak ended where it began. In January 1974, undefeated Notre Dame shocked the top-ranked Bruins in South Bend, Ind., scoring the game's last 12 points to win 71–70. One week later, UCLA would hammer the Irish 94–75 in a rematch, but the damage had been done: UCLA was no longer invincible. In the Final Four, they fell to North Carolina State, and Wooden's streak of seven national titles came to a halt.

The most successful coach in college basketball history, Wooden (below) led UCLA to 10 championships in 12 years.

The Bruins celebrated their 81–76 victory over Florida State for the 1972 national title, their sixth straight.

TIGER SLAM

Let the purists quibble that it wasn't a proper Grand Slam—Tiger Woods's streak of major titles from 2000 to '01 was a feat for the ages.

Those who got caught up in the debate about whether or not Tiger Woods's sweep of the majors—beginning with the 2000 U.S. Open—constituted a Grand Slam missed the point. Grand or not, Woods's slam represented one of the greatest achievements in sports history, not only for what he did, but how he did it.

"What do you have to shoot to win here?" someone asked Stuart Appleby before the 2000 PGA Championship.

"Tiger Woods," was his deadpan reply.

Woods was already the premier player on the tour, but what began at Pebble Beach and culminated at Augusta the following spring was awesome, unprecedented and spectacularly routine. With the exception of the PGA, where he needed three playoff holes to defeat a stubborn Bob May, Woods pasted the finest golfers and golf courses the world has to offer. At Pebble Beach in June, he won by 15 strokes and shot the best score in relation to par in U.S. Open history. At St. Andrews in July, he won by eight strokes and became the youngest man to win a career Grand Slam. And at the Masters, he shot 16-under to spoil the brilliant play of David Duval and win by two strokes. "I kept saying, 'I can't understand why we don't have anyone else playing that well,' " mused Jack Nicklaus. "I am more understanding now. He's that much better."

Nicklaus of course knows a little something about dominance on the golf course. He's won more major tournaments (20) than anyone—for now—and his career has been a measuring stick for Woods since Tiger was a boy. But even the Golden Bear can't say enough about the Tiger. "There are other sports that guys have dominated, but I don't think anybody has dominated an individual sport anywhere near the level he has."

Woods needed the fourth-best Masters score in history to hold off Duval and Phil Mickelson at the 2001 Masters.

In SI's Words

Woods's Sweet Sweep is the most amazing feat we've seen in sports since 1920, when Babe Ruth hit more home runs than every American League team except his New York Yankees. Woods's Mod Quad is the single greatest achievement in golf history, and I don't want to hear another word about Bobby Jones in 1930. You go over to Haggis-on-Bumford and beat three sheep and two guys named Nigel in the British Amateur, you ain't within 1,000 kilometers of winning a fourth major in a row in 2001.

And don't give me any of that "the competition isn't as good now" drivel. Do you realize that David Duval's 14-under-par 274 would've won 59 of the 65 Masters and put him in a playoff in two others? Duval, Phil Mickelson and Ernie Els are all part of the Unlucky Sperm Club, born in the time of the man-eating, trophy-swallowing Cablinasian. They may as well begin studying to be CPAs. They have no chance. They'll never have a chance. What's worse is they now realize that every time they think Woods is slipping, it's only because he's up nights building something even better in the garage.

—*RICK REILLY, APRIL 16, 2001*

3

Although Nicklaus and Arnold Palmer added to the hubbub by publicly stating that Tiger's slam was not a Grand Slam because he didn't win all four tournaments in the same year, there is no denying that Woods hits a golf ball better than anyone who has ever lived. The scary thing is that every time it appears Woods can't get any better, he does, and if the career trajectories of the game's greats are any indication, Woods's best days are still ahead. He may yet win a "true" Grand Slam, making all the controversy of his Tiger Slam a moot point, and he will certainly continue to entrance golf fans. "Someday I'll tell my grandkids I played in the same tournament as Tiger Woods," said Tom Watson, winner of eight majors. "We are witnessing a phenomenon here that the game may never, ever see again."

Woods tracked his birdie putt on 16 at the 2000 PGA Championship, which he won in a three-hole playoff against May.

At the 2000 British Open, Woods safely navigated
St. Andrews' 112 bunkers and won by eight strokes.

2

CELTIC PRIDE

> **The Boston Celtics won 11 titles in 13 years, including eight in a row from 1959 to '66, a string of championships unmatched in any sport.**

THE STOPPER

Despite being blessed with Hall of Famers Elgin Baylor and Jerry West, the Lakers lost seven NBA Finals to the Celtics between 1959 and '69. Three of those series went to a Game 7, yet the Lakers arguably rank second on the list of Celtics foils—to whatever team Wilt Chamberlain was playing for. That's because of the titanic individual rivalry between Chamberlain and Boston's Bill Russell.

When the Celtics' record title run ended in 1967, it was because Chamberlain finally would not be denied. His Philadelphia 76ers went 68–13 that season—the best record in league history at the time—and met the Celtics in the Eastern Division finals. After taking the first three games handily, Philadelphia closed out the series in five. The Sixers then dispatched San Francisco in six to give Chamberlain his first NBA title.

If you thought the Portland Trailblazers' selection of Sam Bowie over Michael Jordan in 1984 was the NBA's greatest draft-day blunder, consider this: In 1956 the Rochester Royals selected Si Green of Duquesne University instead of San Francisco's Bill Russell. No offense to Green, who produced a respectable nine-year career in the league, but Russell formed the cornerstone of the greatest dynasty in professional basketball history. If Jordan is the greatest *player* of all time, then Russell, who guided the Boston Celtics to 11 championships in 13 years, is the greatest *winner* the NBA has ever seen. From 1959 to '66 Russell and the Celtics won eight titles in a row, a feat unmatched in North American professional sports, even by the mighty New York Yankees and Montreal Canadiens.

Assembled and coached by the stogie-smoking iconoclast, Red Auerbach, the Celtics won their first title in 1957 and might have constructed an unbroken string of 10 titles had Russell not sprained his ankle in Game 3 of the '58 Finals, which Boston lost to St. Louis in six games. No matter, the Celtics returned to the championship the following year and began their remarkable streak with a four-game sweep of the Minneapolis Lakers, who would relocate to Los Angeles in 1960 and lose four more Finals to the Celts during Boston's historic run.

Russell was the centerpiece of the Boston squads, but he did not do it alone. He played alongside such Hall of Famers as Bob Cousy, Bill Sharman, K.C. Jones, Tom Heinsohn, Sam Jones and John Havlicek. The streak ended in 1967 with a playoff loss to the Philadelphia 76ers, but Boston came back the following year, with Russell as player-coach, and won it all again.

Auerbach (top right), Russell (third from left) and the Celtics celebrated the 1965 Eastern Division title.

JOLTIN' JOE DIMAGGIO

> *Hitting safely in 56 straight games during the summer of 1941, Joe DiMaggio produced sports' ultimate streak.*

Late in his career, when age and injuries started to take their toll, Joe DiMaggio was asked why he still played so hard every night. "Because," he said, "there might be somebody out there who's never seen me play before." That ethos governed DiMaggio's entire Hall of Fame career, but it was never more evident than in the summer of 1941, when the Yankee Clipper produced his indelible feat, the 56-game hitting streak.

Both DiMaggio and the Yankees started slowly that year. When the streak began on May 15—with a run-scoring single during a 13–1 loss to the Chicago White Sox—Joe D was batting below .300, and New York stood fourth in the American League. But the Yanks and their centerfielder picked up steam after that drubbing. DiMaggio hit safely in the next five games, and on May 24, with his team trailing the Red Sox 6–5, he singled home the winning runs in the bottom of the ninth to stretch his hitting streak to 10 games.

As the string approached 30, it became the talk of the nation. Radio programs were interrupted with daily updates; Les Brown's band hastily recorded a song, "Joltin' Joe DiMaggio," which became a hit; and Bill (Bojangles) Robinson tapdanced atop the Yankees dugout to bring DiMaggio luck.

Suffering insomnia and ulcers under the enormous pressure, Joltin' Joe inched ever closer to the American League record of 41 games, set by the St. Louis Browns' George Sisler in 1922. The major league record—a fact unearthed by baseball officials only that season—was 44, set by Willie Keeler of the Cincinnati Reds in 1897.

When DiMaggio ran his streak to 42 games on June 29, Sisler sent him a telegram that read "I'm glad a real hitter broke it. Keep it up."

Washington fans got a glimpse of DiMaggio's classic stroke as he tied the AL record on June 29 against the Senators.

The consummate all-around star, DiMaggio hit .325 lifetime
and ran the bases almost as well as he patrolled centerfield.

Joe D did keep it up, for 14 more games. He passed Keeler with a three-run homer against the Red Sox on July 2 at Yankee Stadium, and when the streak came to an end, in Cleveland on July 17, it did not go quietly. DiMaggio smoked two hard grounders down the line that Indians third baseman Ken Keltner did well to turn into outs. His mighty streak may have been extinguished, but DiMaggio did not lose his fierce focus. He started another one the next day that lasted 16 games.

After tying Keeler with a single against Boston on July 1, DiMaggio basked in the glow of his accomplishment.

CLOSE CALL

Not surprisingly, Joe DiMaggio had a number of close calls during his record 56-game hitting streak in 1941. There were 34 games in which he kept the streak alive with a single hit, and in nine of those one-hit games, the hit came in his last at bat of the day.

But DiMaggio's two closest calls came in games 30 and 31 of the streak, against the Chicago White Sox. They both involved Dan Daniel, the official scorer at Yankee Stadium. In game 30, DiMaggio, hitless on the day, smacked a routine grounder to shortstop Luke Appling. But the ball took a bad hop and hit the future Hall of Famer in the shoulder. By the time Appling collected the ball and threw to first, he was too late to get DiMaggio. Daniel ruled it a hit, and DiMaggio flied out his next and last time up. The following day DiMaggio hit another grounder—a hard one this time—to Appling. The shortstop could only knock it down, and again Daniel ruled it a hit, allowing the streak to see another day.

INTRODUCTION

"The only completely consistent people," Aldous Huxley wrote in 1929, "are the dead." While we won't take issue with that sentiment, we contend that in the world of sports at least, a select few have come remarkably close to complete consistency—while they were alive, that is, and vibrantly so.

Though they slogged through the occasional off night, the athletes in the following pages possessed an uncanny ability to summon their best almost all of the time, year in and year out. To such metronomic consistency these men added a leathery durability, surpassing talent and, truth be told, a healthy dose of luck—no one avoids serious injury in sports without a bit of good fortune.

Several of the athletes profiled in our "A Lifetime of Excellence" chapter have accomplished feats that could qualify for other sections of the book. Wayne Gretzky's performance in 1982, to name one, was as spectacular as any season in sports history, but these performers didn't stop after one remarkable feat or season: They produced career totals and accomplishments that will live forever in the annals of athletic endeavor.

Yet despite their cream-of-the-crop status—all of them are current or future Hall of Famers—these athletes were not that difficult to rank. Feel free to quibble with our placings, but we stand behind them. We gave special weight to the athlete's level of dominance in his era and to the likelihood of his career feats ever being equaled. Gretzky, then, goes straight to the top. He produced scoring totals that your children's children will not live to see matched, and he ranks with Babe Ruth, Michael Jordan and Muhammad Ali in terms of dominance in his sport and influence, especially in his native Canada.

Gretzky (opposite), Nicklaus (left) and Petty (above) are the measuring sticks for all those who followed them.

A close second to Gretzky is Jack Nicklaus, whose relentless consistency struck fear in the hearts of his opponents and secured 20 major tournament titles, seven more than his nearest competitor. Yes, Tiger Woods is stalking many of the Golden Bear's records and may eventually hunt them down, but that doesn't diminish Nicklaus's achievements. By all appearances, Woods is a once-in-a-century talent—or twice, if you count Nicklaus.

If any fans require proof of Jerry Rice's credentials for the pantheon—though probably none does—they need only consider Rice's 2001 season. At age 39, after the San Francisco 49ers had given up on him as too old, Rice suited up for the Oakland Raiders and caught 83 passes for 1,139 yards. He will retire, when he's good and ready, as the NFL's alltime No. 1 in touchdowns, receptions, receiving yards and combined yards. He's No. 3 on our lifetime-achievement list.

Behind Rice is the indomitable Cy Young, whose 511 career victories are one of sports' untouchable records; Richard Petty, who rides several chassis-lengths ahead of his peers on the NASCAR career victories list; and Hank Aaron, perhaps the quintessential example of sustained excellence. Hammerin' Hank averaged roughly 33 home runs a season for 23 years—back when the home run was not the devalued currency it is today.

For that feat you may argue that Aaron deserves a higher place on our list; you may also claim that the great NHL defenseman Bobby Orr shouldn't be riding in the caboose. But one thing is indisputable: All of these athletes have inspired us with their enduring example, and they've demonstrated that while absolute consistency may be reserved for the hereafter, a lifetime of excellence is attainable—at least for a legend.

12

BEST DEFENSE

Bobby Orr was the NHL's best defenseman a record eight straight times, and his excellence at both ends of the ice revolutionized the sport.

After winning the Norris Trophy as the best defenseman in the NHL in 1967, veteran New York Ranger Harry Howell said, "I'm glad I won it now, because it's going to belong to Orr from now on."

Howell was referring to that season's rookie of the year, 18-year-old Bobby Orr of the Boston Bruins, and he wasn't engaging in hyperbole. Orr would not only win the Norris Trophy in each of the next eight seasons—a record that still stands—he would also reconfigure the game of hockey along the way.

Before the crew-cutted teenager from Parry Sound, Ont., arrived, NHL defensemen played a conservative, stay-at-home style. They concentrated on stopping goals, not creating them. With his blazing speed and deft puckhandling, Orr changed all that. He brought crowds to their feet with his rink-length rushes, and he scored goals almost as often as he set them up. In 1970 he became the first defenseman to lead the NHL in points, with 33 goals and 87 assists.

Orr spearheaded the Bruins' rise from last in the NHL in 1967 to third in the Eastern Division in '68, second in '69 and first in '70, when they won the Stanley Cup for the first time in 29 years. Orr won the Hart (MVP), Ross (scoring champ), Norris and Conn Smythe (playoff MVP) trophies that season, a feat unequaled in the 67-year history of the NHL. He would lead the Bruins to another title in 1972, and though defensemen Paul Coffey and Ray Bourque have surpassed his career point total, Orr's name still comes up first when talk turns to the greatest defensemen of all time.

When Orr arrived in Boston in 1966, the Bruins had not produced a winning season in eight years.

In SI's Words

It's not necessary to get into who may be better, [Bobby] Orr, the defenseman, or Wayne Gretzky, the center, except to note that Orr did something that Gretzky had no opportunity to do, and that was to change the very nature of the game. Before Orr, ice hockey was played on offense by three men, the line. As Orr says matter-of-factly, "My style was to carry the puck"—yes, Mr. Astaire, and was it your style to shuffle your feet?—and in so doing, he converted hockey into all-out offense.

Sometimes, as the seasons passed and I read about Orr doing this or that, I would think back to those late nights when the Boston sportswriters talked of his coming and how it would be for the Bruins, and it was eerie. At least for me, there has never been anyone in sport dressed in such inevitability as Bobby Orr.

—FRANK DEFORD, AUGUST 5, 1985

11

GRAND ENCORE

> **In the history of tennis, only two men have won the Grand Slam. Rod Laver accomplished the feat twice, in 1962 and 1969.**

In 1962 Rod Laver duplicated Don Budge's 1938 Grand Slam by winning Wimbledon, and the U.S., French and Australian opens in the same year. Only Budge had done it before, and only one man would do it again. Seven years later, Laver repeated his Slam at the tennis-ripe age of 31, staking his claim to the title of greatest player in tennis history.

Although Laver was nicknamed Rocket, the modest 5' 8", 145-pound redhead was not imposing—until you saw him fire laser-like serves past a hapless opponent as he often did. On the court, he was a demon. "If I'm in trouble, I attack," Laver said. "Better to put more pressure on the other player."

But Laver wasn't satisfied with just winning amateur tournaments. After defeating Roy Emerson in four sets at the 1962 U.S. Open to complete his first Grand Slam, Laver turned professional, thus disqualifying himself from the four major tournaments for five of his prime years. "I wanted to play the best," Laver said. "I wanted to know, 'Am I No. 1 or No. 4.' " Early on, the professionals handled Laver, but he was a quick study. By the time the last major tournament began admitting professionals, in 1969, Laver boasted the greatest combination of power and precision the game had ever seen. "I went to Australia with [the Slam] in mind," he admitted. He won 31 straight matches during one stretch that year and dropped only two sets in the four Grand Slam finals. Laver ranks third on the alltime list for most major singles titles, but his two Grand Slams set him apart. "That's why he's arguably the best ever," says Pete Sampras, the alltime leader in Grand Slam singles titles. "He's won on all surfaces, and he did it twice."

Laver defeated fellow Australian John Newcombe in four sets to win his fourth Wimbledon title and the 1969 Grand Slam.

In SI's Words

When Laver is behind, he appears to be—he *is*—more dangerous; when he is forced into the extremes of the court, into the corners, he has an astonishing faculty for drawing back and ripping through his best shots. There is a suspicion around that he is only at his best when he is behind and has to rally. He seems always to be making it back from 15–40, or two sets to love. . . .

There are moments when Laver's brilliance on the court is so sharply defined, so beautifully conceived, that the witness of it crowds a man's throat with pleasure and even the most sophisticated tennis audience is heard to gurgle and ahhh.

—JOHN UNDERWOOD, MAY 31, 1971

10

THE BROCKTON BRAWLER

> *His style may have been primitive and his reign relatively brief, but Rocky Marciano retired as the only unbeaten heavyweight champion.*

Rocky Marciano of Brockton, Mass., lacked many of the ideal physical traits of a heavyweight champion. "He was too old [when he took up boxing], almost 25," said trainer Goody Petronelli. "He was too short, he was too light. He had no reach. Rough and tough, but no finesse." But what the Rock lacked in physical presence he made up for in tenacity and ferocity to become the only undefeated champion in heavyweight history.

Boxing promoter Al Weill teamed the 5' 10", 190-pound Marciano with veteran trainer Charley Goldman, who taught the fighter his signature crouch-and-lunge style. When he turned pro in 1948, Marciano immediately displayed the power and durable chin that would guide him to a 35–0 record.

In 1951 Marciano had his first big test, against Rex Layne, another heavy hitter. Layne lasted only six rounds, falling beneath a barrage of body punches. Later that year Marciano squared off against an aging Joe Louis. In a mismatch, he dispatched the slower ex-champ in eight rounds and earned his first title shot. Though many fight aficionados didn't give Marciano and his primitive, brawling style much of a chance against the crafty champ, Jersey Joe Walcott, Marciano once again proved them wrong by knocking Walcott cold in the 13th round to claim the heavyweight crown.

Marciano defended his title six times between 1952 and 1955, including two ferocious battles with former champ Ezzard Charles. His final defense came against Archie Moore on September 21, 1955. It ended in predictable fashion, with Marciano scoring a ninth-round KO. Not wanting to join the long list of fighters who stuck around too long, Marciano retired in April 1956 at the age of 32. Unlike most boxers, his first retirement was also his last retirement, preserving an unblemished record of 49–0 (43 KOs) that remains unequaled.

In SI's Words

Marciano was an enormously popular champion, and more than his complexion lay at the source of the appeal. The archetypal working-class stiff from blue-collar Brockton, he brought to the lights a boxing style edited down to its barest essentials, an unearthly power of will and tolerance for punishment, particularly around the chin; and he had what columnist Red Smith called "a right hand that registered nine on the Richter scale," and a left hook that trembled the upright like an aftershock. Stir into this mix an incomparable appetite for work, a quality of meekness and humility that was often affecting—after knocking out his boyhood idol, Joe Louis, in the eighth round of their 1951 fight in New York, Marciano wept openly in Louis's locker room—and that crooked smile on a darkly handsome mug, and what you had was the ideal composite for the central character in a cartoonlike Hollywood movie.
—WILLIAM NACK, AUGUST 23, 1993

Three months after their first meeting, Marciano (right) knocked out Charles in the eighth round to retain his title.

9

LOUISIANA LIGHTNING

> *In three seasons at Louisiana State, Pete Maravich averaged 44.2 points per game and topped the NCAA career scoring list.*

Pete Maravich was born and raised to play basketball, and for three magic years at Louisiana State, he was a one-man highlight show. Sporting his trademark floppy hair and drooping socks, Pistol Pete thrilled fans with a dazzling arsenal of offense. His artistry, passion and creativity combined to make him the greatest scorer the college game has ever seen. He scored at least 50 points in a game 28 times and graduated as the highest scorer in NCAA history, with 3,667 points.

Maravich had basketball in his genes. His father, Press, was a college coach and played an active role in his son's development. "By age 13, the basketball had become an extension of me and my personality," said Maravich. So it wasn't a surprise that Maravich joined his dad at LSU following an outstanding high school career. After toying with the freshman team in his first year, Maravich led the nation in scoring as a sophomore. The Tigers lacked depth, and Press gave his son free rein to display his talents. In the era before the three-point shot and the shot clock, Maravich piled up scoring totals that jumped out of the boxscore.

UCLA coach John Wooden called Maravich the best ballhandler he had ever seen, and his passing skills—although often underused—were brilliant. But his teams never won a championship, and some critics derided LSU's lack of teamwork. "He scores a lot of points, but he creates just as many," argued Press. Maravich never blinked—or stopped shooting. If the Tigers weren't winning titles, at least they were the greatest show around. LSU sold out arenas across the country, and their coach was just another fan. "I get to the point where I don't coach him," said Press. "I just watch."

Maravich scored 64 points against Kentucky in 1970, but the Wildcats won the game 121–105.

8

THE RIGHT HAND OF AMERICA

During a crucial period of our nation's history, Joe Louis's 12-year rule as heavyweight champ made him a hero to all Americans.

Joe Louis was heavyweight champion for so long that an entire generation of boxing fans could not remember when that was not so. In 1937 when Louis was only 23, he became the youngest man to win the heavyweight championship, knocking out James Braddock in the eighth round. He went on to defend his title 25 times over a record 12-year reign.

There had not been a black heavyweight champion since Jack Johnson, whose flamboyant behavior out of the ring tested the racial mores of the early 1900s. Not much had changed when Louis began his professional career in 1934 and won his first 27 fights. Segregation and racial prejudices still permeated almost every facet of American life, including the media. The press tagged him with a slew of racially-insensitive nicknames including the Dark Destroyer and the Brown Bomber. With quiet resolve, Louis continued to KO his competition, before suffering a devastating loss to Germany's Max Schmeling in 1936—an outcome which Adolf Hitler embraced as evidence of Aryan supremacy.

Undeterred, Louis came back to win the heavyweight title from Braddock on June 22, 1937. One year later, in an eagerly anticipated rematch, he avenged his only loss by knocking out Schmeling in the first round. The entire country, black and white, was galvanized by Louis's victory, and Jimmy Cannon wrote, "Joe Louis is a credit to his race . . . the human race."

Louis beat future champ Jersey Joe Walcott twice in a span of seven months in 1948, before retiring as champion in 1950. His rule over the heavyweight division was defined as much by its longevity and number of defenses as by what Louis came to mean to a people and a country. As Jesse Jackson eloquently said at Louis's funeral: "Usually, the champion rides on the shoulders of the nation . . . but in this case the nation rode on the shoulders of the hero."

MOUNTAINTOP

On the brink of his highly anticipated rematch with Max Schmeling, Joe Louis found himself part prize fighter and part political pawn. He did not disappoint in either capacity.

On June 22, 1938, in front of 70,000 fans at Yankee Stadium, Joe Louis wasted little time going after the man dubbed the "Heil Hitler Hero" by the press. Thirty seconds into the fight, Louis nailed Schmeling with a right hand shot that cracked a bone in Schmeling's spine. Unable to lift his left arm, Schmeling never had a chance. Louis dropped him three times, and the bout lasted all of 124 seconds.

In winning this historic fight, Louis not only redeemed his lone loss as a professional, but also struck a symbolic blow for democracy against the tide of fascism that would ultimately draw the United States into World War II.

Louis punished Lou Nova for six rounds in 1941 before the fight was stopped. Overall, Louis was 63–3 with 49 KOs.

SEVENTH HEAVEN

Some of the greatest pitchers in the Hall of Fame never threw even one no-hitter. Nolan Ryan tossed seven in his spectacular career.

Outfielder Oscar Gamble once described a good day at the plate against Nolan Ryan as "0 for 4 and not getting hit in the head." A 6' 2" righthander with a 95-plus mph fastball, Ryan inspired many a nightmare for opposing hitters. Intimidation played a significant role in each of Ryan's record seven no-hitters, which are three more than any other pitcher has thrown.

Ryan was a threat to throw a no-hitter every time he took the mound. Upon joining the California Angels in 1972, he quickly made a name for himself by striking out a league-leading 329. The following year, he won 21 games, whiffed a record 383 batters, and hurled his first two no-hitters. During his second no-hitter, Ryan was so overpowering that Detroit's Norm Cash jokingly came to the plate toting a table leg instead of a bat, figuring he'd have just as good a shot at making contact. Ryan added a third no-hitter in 1974 and a fourth in 1975 that tied Sandy Koufax's major league record.

He signed as a free agent with Houston before the 1980 season, and one year later the 34-year-old Texan had the record all to himself after he blanked Koufax's former club, the Los Angeles Dodgers, 5–0. Ryan completed his stellar 27-year career with the Texas Rangers, for whom he pitched two more no-hitters and ran his career win total to 324. His seventh and final no-hitter came in 1991, when, at age 44, he blanked Toronto 3–0. Don't feel too bad for the hitters, though. They occasionally scratched out a hit against Ryan, as his 12 career one-hitters will attest.

After four uneventful seasons with the New York Mets, Ryan became a superstar with the California Angels.

MOUNTAINTOP

In 1989, at the age of 42, Nolan Ryan of the Texas Rangers was still baseball's premier power pitcher. He was already the all-time major league strikeout leader and needed just 225 more K's to reach the seemingly unsurpassable number of 5,000.

Pitching for the Rangers on a hot August night in Arlington, Texas, Ryan faced the Oakland A's, needing just six strikeouts to reach the milestone. A crowd of 42,869, including Rangers' owner George W. Bush, turned out to witness history. After fanning five A's in the first four innings, Ryan faced Rickey Henderson to start off the fifth. Down to his last strike, Henderson whiffed on a blistering 96-mph fastball.

After the game, a 2–0 Texas loss in which Ryan whiffed 13 A's, Henderson summed up Ryan's accomplishment perfectly, saying "It was an honor to be the 5,000th. As [Rangers' coach] Davey Lopes says, 'If he ain't struck you out, you ain't nobody.' "

6

HAMMERIN' HANK

Eclipsing a legend wasn't easy, but the dignity Hank Aaron exhibited while hitting 755 home runs made him one of the alltime greats.

MOUNTAINTOP

Baseball fans always look forward to Opening Day, and in April 1974 they had even greater cause for excitement: Hank Aaron started the season only one home run short of Babe Ruth's career record of 714.

In Cincinnati, Aaron hit one out with his first swing of the season to draw even with Ruth. He played sparingly in the next two games, as Braves manager Eddie Mathews did everything he could to make sure Aaron didn't break the record on the road. Fortunately for Braves fans, all the balls he hit stayed in the park.

The Braves returned to Atlanta on April 8 to face the Dodgers. Los Angeles's Al Downing walked Aaron in his first at bat, but he couldn't dodge number 44 the next time. In the fourth inning, Downing delivered a high fastball that Aaron smashed over the left centerfield wall. As the stadium erupted in celebration, fans raced onto the field and chased Aaron around third base. His typically understated response: "Right now, it feels just like another home run. I just wanted to touch all the bases on this one."

Hank Aaron approached Babe Ruth's home run record the same way he approached everything in his life: quietly. Aaron always did things at his own pace, and he seemed to view reaching the record as nothing more than a part of his job. The steadiness of his character was reflected in his extraordinary consistency at the plate. For 23 years Aaron averaged nearly 33 home runs a year, yet he never hit more than 47 in a season. When he finally retired in 1976, Aaron had hit more home runs than any man in Major League Baseball history.

It is difficult to separate Aaron's career from its historical context. He began his professional career in 1952 with the Indianapolis Clowns of the Negro League, and his career unfolded along with the civil rights movement. As a minor leaguer in the Deep South, Aaron encountered racial prejudices that would shadow his career but helped him forge the quiet, dignified approach that was to prove his greatest asset in the majors.

Once he joined the Milwaukee Braves in 1954, Aaron demonstrated the sweet stroke that earned him two batting titles and four home run crowns. Still, many fans were surprised when it became glaringly obvious in 1973 that Aaron was going to break Ruth's record. Some Americans did not want a black man to break the record, and others could not conceive that someone they perceived as ordinary would eclipse the larger-than-life Ruth. They tainted Aaron's pursuit of the record with hundreds of angry and bigoted letters. "It should have been the most enjoyable time in my life," said Aaron. "And instead it was hell."

In the end, the letters were about as effective as the opposing pitchers. Aaron continued to hit and the records continued to fall. In addition to the home run record, he set career records for runs batted in and total bases. Twenty-eight years after his historic number 715, Aaron's records still stand—a tribute to sustained excellence, hard work and humility.

In 1957 Aaron led the National League in home runs (44) and RBIs (132) and helped the Braves win the World Series.

5

KING OF THE ROAD

> *Richard Petty won 200 races—nearly twice as many as anyone else—and helped turn a Southern sport into a national passion.*

Richard Petty is racing royalty and he has the title to prove it. In NASCAR circles, he is known simply as The King, and the cowboy hat, sunglasses and mustache underlined by his wide grin are as recognizable as any corporate logo. Petty and NASCAR grew up together, and nearly two decades after his last victory, he remains one of the sport's most popular personalities. It is a reputation he cultivated during a lifetime of racing, from the dusty dirt tracks near his home in Level Cross, N.C., to the banked turns of the Daytona Superspeedway where he won a record seven Daytona 500s. "Richard was made for this sport," said driver Darrell Waltrip. "Or this sport was made for Richard, however you want to look at it."

No one has taken more checkered flags than Richard Petty. Then again, no driver has raced as often or for as long. Petty benefited from a willingness to race anytime, anywhere. "He raced large and small tracks, even some places where there were no tracks at all," said longtime NASCAR reporter Benny Phillips. During his 35-year career, Petty won 200 of 1,184 races. To put those numbers in perspective, David Pearson, NASCAR's second alltime winningest driver, trails the King by 95 victories, and no active driver has more than 58 wins. NASCAR's reigning star, Jeff Gordon, would have to maintain his current level of success for two more decades to approach Petty's record.

But Petty did not make history simply by outlasting his contemporaries. He dominated the competition. In addition to his seven Daytona 500 wins, Petty won seven Winston Cup titles, a record matched only by the late Dale Earnhardt. In 1967 he won 27 races, including a

Petty won more than $8 million in his 35-year racing career.

MOUNTAINTOP

Twenty-four years after his first NASCAR victory, Richard Petty won his last. At Daytona, on the Fourth of July, two days after his 47th birthday, with President Reagan among the 80,000 fans in attendance, Petty won the Firecracker 400 for his 200th career victory. It was the final coronation of Petty's career, and the circumstances befit the man who had carried the sport on his shoulders for so long. Becoming the oldest man to win a NASCAR race, Petty inched past Cale Yarborough on Lap 157 to beat him to a caution flag by less than half a car length. "It was definitely one of those storybook deals," said Petty. "It's July Fourth and this [guy's] been trying to win his 200th race. Then he does it on virtually the last lap. Hollywood wouldn't believe it."

record 10 in a row. His triumphs won headlines and helped put
NASCAR in the national spotlight.

Some critics claim that Petty's unrivaled success was the result of a
superior car, not superior driving skills, but Bobby Allison, one of
Petty's great rivals, admired Petty's grit: "He went to every event as
long and strong and hard as he could go." For his part, Petty said, "I
never claimed to be the best driver. I just want to be remembered as a
winner." That will never be in doubt.

Petty (above, 43) won his sixth
Daytona 500 in 1979 after
Cale Yarborough and Donnie
Allison wrecked on the last lap.

His easygoing personality made
Petty (below) a fan favorite.
"Anybody else who tried to
come in . . . had to be the bad
guy," said Darrell Waltrip.

THE PITCHER OF RECORD

Cy Young's record of 511 career victories will never be broken, and his name has been immortalized to define pitching excellence.

When Denton True Young tried out for the Canton, Ohio, team in the Tri-State League in 1890, he threw with such power that some of his pitches damaged the wooden grandstand behind home plate. The batter he was facing declared that the structure "looked like a cyclone had hit it," and thus the legend of Cy—short for Cyclone—Young was born. He was nicknamed for a natural phenomenon, and the career path of Young's storm tore up the baseball record book.

In a career that spanned 22 seasons, Young had five 30-win seasons and 10 20-win seasons. Altogether he won 511 games, almost 100 more than his closest rival. The number is far beyond what is considered attainable by modern ballplayers, causing some to doubt the validity of the record and the level of Young's competition. Baseball has changed since Young began playing. The pitching mound has been moved farther away from home plate, and the ball has been wound tighter to generate greater offense. But as Young pointed out, whatever advantages the state of the game accorded him, he also "played on poor fields, with poor equipment, ate bad food, had bad travel conditions." Whatever the conditions, it is impossible to deny that Young was an extraordinary pitcher.

No one has seriously challenged Young's career win record, and it is doubtful that anyone ever will. The adoption of five-man pitching rotations limits the number of starts for even the best of pitchers, and the introduction of relief specialists costs starting pitchers additional victories. If a pitcher were to average 20 wins a season for 20 years, he would be a shoo-in for the Hall of Fame. But he would still be 111 victories behind the Cyclone.

During his career with Cleveland, St. Louis and Boston, Young completed 749 of the 815 games he started.

EPILOGUE

Cy Young is best known today for the pitching award that is named in his honor. The Cy Young Award has been given to the game's best pitchers since 1956. But there was another Cy Young award, and it may have been a greater testament to Young's legacy. In 1908, American League players chipped in to buy a commemorative cup for Young, who was approaching the end of his career in Boston. The inscription read: "From the ball players of the American League to show their appreciation of Cy Young, as a man and as a ball player. August 13, 1908."

3

NO FINER NINER

Jerry Rice has caught more passes (1,364) and scored more touch-downs (195) than any other football player—and he's not done yet.

Jerry Rice plays football at a different speed. But when he first entered the NFL, many scouts doubted if he had any speed at all. Rice's 40-yard dash time at the 1985 scouting combine was so ordinary that many teams gave up on him. But stopwatches couldn't measure Rice's game speed. "Every time he catches it, there is a good chance he could end up scoring," said general manager Bobby Beathard, who built Super Bowl teams in Washington and San Diego. "I'd like to know what his speed is over the 40 yards once he catches the ball." Teams would spend the next two decades regretting their decision not to select the receiver from Mississippi Valley State, as Rice became the sport's alltime greatest touchdown scorer.

The third receiver picked in the 1985 draft, Rice made an immediate impact with the San Francisco 49ers, a championship-caliber team with a championship-caliber passing game. After scoring four touchdowns and racking up 927 yards as a rookie, he took the league by storm in 1986, torching opposing secondaries for an NFL-best 15 TD receptions. A labor strike shortened the 1987 season, but Rice still scored 23 touch-downs in 12 games. His 22 touchdown catches and 138 points were the most ever by a wide receiver. During the next nine years Rice averaged over 13 touchdowns and more than 1,400 receiving yards per season.

And his brilliance was not limited to the regular season. In three Super Bowls, all San Francisco victories, Rice set the record for most career touchdowns (7) and points (42). He was named MVP of Super Bowl XXIII and still has designs on returning to the big game. In 2001 Rice crossed the Bay to play for the Oakland Raiders. At age 39 he scored nine more TDs, raising his career mark to 195. With 200 well within his surehanded grasp, Rice shows no signs of slowing down, no matter what the stopwatch reads.

In SI's Words

Afield, as in life, Rice is evasive. He almost never takes a direct, crushing blow after catching a pass. He controls his body like a master puppeteer working a marionette. A one-handed grab here, a tiptoe up the sideline there, an unscathed sprint through two closing safeties when it seems decapitation is imminent.

"I don't think I've ever seen him all stretched out," says 49er quarterback Steve Young of Rice's ability to avoid big hits. Rice jumps only when he has to, and unlike almost all other receivers, he catches passes in mid-stride and effortlessly continues running, the ball like a sprinter's baton in his hand. . . .

And the hands. Clad in gloves, the hands are so supple and sure that last year they snared a touchdown pass by latching onto the tail end of a fading ball. "That was not giving up on the ball," explains Rice. Sounds simple. In reality it's like grabbing the back end of a greased pig.

—*RICK TELANDER, FEBRUARY 16, 1995*

Rice has gained 1,000 or more yards in a season 13 times in his career, and he has caught 100 or more passes four times.

THE GOLD STANDARD

Between 1959 and 1986, Jack Nicklaus won a record 20 major tournaments, setting a standard by which all other golfers are measured.

In 1959, a burly, square-headed 19-year old from Ohio birdied the final hole at Broadmoor to win the United States Amateur title. Twenty-seven years later, a presumed has-been with the same name blazed the back nine at Augusta with a 30, to win his sixth green jacket. In between those two landmark victories, Jack Nicklaus won 18 other major tournaments, seven more than Bobby Jones, whose record of 13 had stood for more than 40 years.

Jones himself famously trumpeted the Age of Nicklaus during the 1965 Masters when he said, "Jack plays a game with which I am not familiar." Whether he was the Fat Jack who drew the wrath of golfing fans simply for conquering the beloved Arnold Palmer, or the Golden Bear whose consistency and competitive drive dominated two decades of golf, Nicklaus's talent and versatility were never in doubt. He out-hit the competition, launching mammoth tee shots that turned the lengthiest of par fives into bird or even eagle sanctuaries. He out-thought them: "I learned more about course management from watching Jack than all the other pros combined," said Tom Watson, who jousted with Nicklaus in several classic duels in the late 1970s. And if Nicklaus's formidable skills weren't enough, his reputation alone could intimidate the competition. "He knows he's going to win," said Tom Weiskopf, another champion sentenced to play in Nicklaus's long shadow. "You know he's going to win. And he knows that you know he's going to win." The mere sight of the name "Nicklaus" on a leaderboard was enough to make the most professional of golfers suffer meltdowns.

After winning another amateur title in 1961, Nicklaus defeated Palmer in an 18-hole playoff to win the 1962 U.S. Open at Oakmont. He won three of the next four Masters championships (1963, '65 and

In 1968 at Oak Hill, Nicklaus just missed becoming the first man to win back-to-back U.S. Opens since Ben Hogan.

In SI's Words

There is not a shingle missing in his brilliant career. He won where he was supposed to win: Augusta and Firestone (six times each), Pebble Beach (four), St. Andrews and Baltusrol (twice each), Oakmont, Muirfield. He won on Tour 70 times. He won every major at least three times; nobody else has won every major even twice. Yet it wasn't easy. He began as a hero with no home, showing up at the 1962 Open at Oakmont—his first U.S. Open as a pro—looking like something you might pull from the bottom pouch of your golf bag. Fat and rumpled and wearing a dorky rain hat, his task was to conquer the beloved Arnie and his Army, who booed Nicklaus's good shots and yelled, "Miss it, Jack!" on the putting green. He beat Palmer 71–74 in an 18-hole playoff at that Open, and golf was never the same. He was not homespun like Sam Snead, not funny like Trevino. His pants didn't need hitching like Palmer's. Instead, he won over America with pure, unbleached excellence.

—RICK REILLY, SEPTEMBER 19, 1994

'66), and at age 26 he became only the fourth golfer to win a career Grand Slam when he won his first British Open at Muirfield. When he won his 20th and arguably his most memorable major—the 1986 Masters—Nicklaus had accumulated the equivalent of three career Grand Slams: six Masters, five PGAs, four U.S. Opens, and three British Opens. In comparison, Palmer and Gary Player, Nicklaus's two chief rivals, *combined* for 17 major titles.

As impressive as Nicklaus's victory total is, with just a few shots and a few more lucky bounces it could have been even better. He placed second at a major tournament 19 times and had 17 other Top 5 finishes. But Nicklaus isn't remembered for how many times he finished second. Nicklaus was a champion, and his will to win was unequaled— perhaps in any sport. "For Jack, everything is a challenge," said Chi-Chi Rodriguez. Nicklaus pursued perfection, and in the end, he settled for greatness.

Nicklaus combined sheer power off the tee with a deft touch around the green (left) that made him one of the game's greatest clutch putters. At the 1972 U.S. Open at Pebble Beach (right), he overcame windy conditions to win his third title.

THE GREAT ONE

> *Wayne Gretzky's career may be the greatest body of work in sports history, and his record for career points will last several lifetimes.*

Choosing an angle from which to approach Wayne Gretzky, we feel the way he must have felt during his prime, with the puck on his stick: The options are limitless. Do you start with his extraordinary statistics, his uncanny passing ability or his silky elusiveness? How about the way he utterly dominated the NHL despite his lack of size, strength and speed? You could begin with his unerring good grace as hockey's greatest ambassador, or with his child-prodigy early days, which earned him his famous nickname.

Canadians started calling Gretzky the Great One when he was 10 years old, after he scored 378 goals in 68 games for his Brantford, Ont., youth team. In fact, they'd known about him for years. At five he was playing against 10- and 11-year-olds. At eight he was the subject of a Toronto *Globe and Mail* feature. At nine he made an appearance on national television after he scored 105 goals as a defenseman. At 16 Gretzky led the World Junior Championships in scoring and became a bona fide national hero.

All of which points up one of his greatest and most overlooked accomplishments. On display and hyped beyond reason since childhood, he not only met the outsized expectations others had for him, but exceeded them. That feat, achieved under enormous pressure, ranks with the 92 goals he scored in the 1981–82 NHL season, or the 163 assists he racked up in 1985–86.

Indeed, his dominance in the NHL was almost as complete as it had been at the youth level. No one had ever cracked 200 points in a season before Gretzky did in 1981–82, and no one, except Gretzky, has done it since. He *averaged* 203 points a year for six consecutive seasons. Not coincidentally, his Edmonton Oilers went to four Stanley Cups during

Gretzky led the Oilers to the 1983 Stanley Cup finals, setting playoff records for assists (26) and points (38).

EPILOGUE

When Gretzky retired in 1999, there was only honor missing from his résumé: an Olympic gold medal. Canada had not won Olympic gold in hockey since 1952, and Gretzky's own dreams of gold had ended in the semifinals of the 1998 Nagano Games. Nevertheless, he was Canada's choice for executive director of the 2002 team, and he dedicated himself to ending his country's 50-year drought. Gretzky's selections for the national team bruised some egos, and the team's poor play in the round-robin phase of the tournament threatened to turn the Great One into a great goat. Gretzky went on the offensive, attacking the media for what he perceived as its bias against Canada. His surprising outburst helped turn the Canadians around, and they defeated the host Americans 5–2 in the gold medal game. "That was Wayne Gretzky talking," said Canada defenseman Al MacInnis. "Over the last 25 years, no one has meant more to the sport or the country. He was showing us that he was just as emotional as a management figure as he was on the ice."

that span, winning three. A nine-time league MVP, Gretzky won four Cups in all with Edmonton, and when he was traded to the Los Angeles Kings in 1988, Canadians felt something like Americans would feel if the Statue of Liberty had been dealt to Italy.

Gretzky has more goals (894) than any player in NHL history, and if you took them all away, he would still top the NHL's alltime points list on the strength of his 1,963 assists. But unfortunately for the competition, the goals count, and they give the Great One a record 2,857 career points. Halley's Comet will reappear before anyone tops that total. Gretzky beat the hype from wire to wire. Talk about a lifetime of excellence.

Although he won four Stanley Cups as an Edmonton Oiler, Gretzky broke the NHL's career goals record with the Los Angeles Kings (above), and he played his last professional game for the New York Rangers (left).

HONORABLE MENTION

UNTOUCHABLE
The greatest pitching performance in World Series history occurred in 1905, when Christy Mathewson of the New York Giants threw three shutouts in six days to help defeat the Philadelphia Athletics in five games. In 27 innings of work, Mathewson struck out 18 A's and allowed only 14 hits.

THE GREATEST ATHLETE
At the 1912 Olympics in Stockholm, competing in his first decathlon, Jim Thorpe easily won the gold medal with a performance so far ahead of its time it would have won silver at the 1948 Olympics. In 1950 the Associated Press named him the greatest athlete of the first half of the 20th century.

FLYING FINN
Paavo Nurmi won nine gold medals during his Olympic career, but his greatest performance may have been at the 1924 Games in Paris. Thirty minutes after winning the 1,500 meters, he set an Olympic record in the 5,000 meters.

BABE WATCH
At the 1932 AAU Championships, Babe Didrikson (below) was a one-woman team. Literally. As the only member of the team representing the Dallas insurance company at which

she worked, Didrikson single-handedly won the national championship by taking five of the eight events she entered, setting three world records in the process.

KING CARL
On July 10, 1934, Carl Hubbell of the New York Giants baffled a series of future Hall of Famers with his screwball. In two innings of work at the All-Star Game, Hubbell whiffed Babe Ruth, Lou Gehrig, Jimmie Foxx, Al Simmons and Joe Cronin.

BEAR TRAP
The Chicago Bears avenged a 7–3 loss to the Washington Redskins during the regular season by humbling the Skins 73–0 in the 1940 NFL Championship. It remains the greatest rout in league history.

SIMPLY PERFECT
Yankees pitcher Don Larsen, who never won more games in a season than the 11 he won in 1956, retired all 27 Brooklyn Dodgers he faced in Game 5 of the '56 World Series. New York won the series in seven games, and Larsen's gem is the only perfect game in postseason history.

MR. OCTOBER
Yankee Stadium. The 1977 World Series. Game 6. When Reggie Jackson slammed home runs on three consecutive swings against the Los Angeles Dodgers, he clinched New York's first World Series championship since 1962 and earned his famous moniker.

PISTON POWER
In the fifth and deciding game of a first-round playoff series against the New York Knicks in 1984, the Detroit Pistons' Isiah Thomas scored 16 points in the final 94 seconds of the fourth quarter to force overtime. Thomas's great feat went for naught, though, as the Knicks won 127–123.

BOOM-BOOM
In 1985 unseeded 17-year-old Boris Becker blasted 21 aces past Kevin Curren in a four-set final to become the youngest men's Wimbledon champion in history. For good measure, he became the second-youngest Wimbledon champ when he successfully defended his title in 1986.

LET IT RYDE

Trailing by four points heading into the final day of the 1999 Ryder Cup competition, the U.S. team won eight of Sunday's 12 single matches and tied one to stun the Europeans. Justin Leonard's 45-foot putt on the 17th hole set off a wild celebration on the green, but it wasn't until José María Olazábal missed his own 20-footer that American victory was assured.

DUELING ACES

In 1968—the same year Denny McLain won 31 games—Bob Gibson of the St. Louis Cardinals dominated the National League with a 1.12 ERA, the lowest single-season ERA since 1914. In Game 1 of the World Series, he struck out 17 Detroit Tigers.

BO KNOWS ALL-STAR GAMES

For a brief moment in time, Bo Jackson (above) was America's biggest sports star. In 1989, as an outfielder for the Kansas City Royals, he hit 32 home runs and was named the MVP of the All-Star Game. In 1990 he rushed for 698 yards in 10 games for the Los Angeles Raiders and was elected to the NFL Pro Bowl. A hip injury, sadly, would curtail his careers in both sports.

SACK MASTER

On Nov. 11, 1990, Derrick Thomas of the Kansas City Chiefs sacked Seattle's quarterback, Dave Krieg, a record seven times. On the last play of the game, however, Thomas narrowly missed his eighth sack, enabling Krieg to throw a last-second touchdown pass for a Seahawk victory.

ROCKET MAN

Ten years after setting the major-league record with 20 strike-outs in a single game, Roger Clemens of the Boston Red Sox did it again, whiffing 20 Detroit Tigers, on Sept. 18, 1996.

THE RUNNING OF THE BILL

Long before his infamous murder trial, O.J. Simpson was the best running back in the NFL. In 1973, as a member of the Buffalo Bills, Simpson became the first running back to surpass 2,000 yards in a season when he ran for 2,003. He remains the only man to have reached that milestone in 14 games.

PHIL-ING UP THE NET

Phil Esposito of the Boston Bruins shattered the NHL record for goals in a single season, scoring 76 of them in 1970–71. Espo, who surpassed Bobby Hull's mark by 18 goals, also set the NHL record for points (152). Both milestones lasted until a guy named Gretzky came along.

FRÄULEIN FOREHAND

Four other tennis players have won the Grand Slam, but only Steffi Graf's 1988 Slam is "Golden." Graf swept the four major tournaments and added an Olympic gold medal at the Seoul Summer Games.

PASSING FANCY

Calling the signals for college football's top offense in 1990, David Klingler of the University of Houston achieved one feat after another. Against Eastern Washington, he threw 11 touchdown passes; against Arizona State, he threw for 716 yards. Both stats are NCAA records. For the season, Klingler passed for 5,140 yards in 11 games, an average of 467 yards a game, and another NCAA record.

OREL SURGEON

Los Angeles's Orel Hershiser didn't allow a run for 59 regular-season innings in 1988. Throw in his first playoff start against the New York Mets, and he went 67 innings—the equivalent of more than seven straight shutouts—without yielding a run.

HAIL, CAEL

Cael Sanderson (above) of Iowa State became the first college wrestler to go undefeated in college and win four NCAA titles. His victory against Jon Trenge of Lehigh in the 2002 NCAA Championship ran his streak of victories to 159.

GOAL ORIENTED

The University of North Carolina might be best known for its men's basketball team, but Dean Smith can't compete with Anson Dorrance's record as head coach of the school's women's soccer team. His Tar Heels won 16 NCAA titles—including nine in a row from '86 to '94—in 20 years.

THE GREAT RAJAH

It's been more than 60 years since a baseball player hit .400 in a season, making St. Louis Cardinals second baseman Rogers Hornsby's feat that much more impressive. From 1921 to '25, Hornsby hit an astonishing .402, including a major league record .424 in 1924.

G-OH-ING, GONE

The international home run king is Sadaharu Oh of Japan, who hit 868 home runs during his career with the Tokyo Giants. Although he played in smaller ballparks than his American counterparts, he also played in seasons of only 130 games. As a result, he hit 113 more career home runs than Hank Aaron in 3,000 fewer at bats.

EVERY ROSE HAS ITS THORN

Pete Rose remains banned from baseball and from the Hall of Fame, but his reign as the Hit King is undisputed. He eclipsed Ty Cobb in 1985 and retired with 4,256 hits in 24 major league seasons.

UKRAINIAN SENSATION

For more than a decade, Sergei Bubka of the Ukraine ruled the pole vault, setting 35 world records. In 1983, as a citizen of the Soviet Union, he won the first of six consecutive world championships.

MAMA MIA

No player—male or female—has scored more international soccer goals than Mia Hamm of the United States. A member of the national team since the age of 15, Hamm has netted 129 goals in 219 games through 2001.

ST. PATRICK

Patrick Roy (right) was ......int on or off the ice, but t........ ..f the Montreal ....e Colorado Avalanche ...found themselves counting on him for a crucial victory. A three-time winner of the Conn S........ hy, which is awarded ....anley Cup playoffs,

Roy finished the 2001–02 season as the NHL's alltime leader in victories (516).

JAZZ ARTIST

No basketball player in the history of the NBA has been better at setting up his teammates than John Stockton of the Utah Jazz. In 18 years with the Jazz, the 6' 1" guard from Gonzaga University has 15,177 assists (and counting), more than 5,000 ahead of Magic Johnson.

PHOTO CREDITS

FRONT COVER
Clockwise from left: Bettmann/CORBIS; John W. McDonough; John Biever; Paul J. Bereswill.

BACK COVER
From left: Walter Iooss Jr.; James Drake; Mike Powell/Allsport.

FRONT MATTER
1, Walter Iooss Jr.; 2-3, Walter Iooss Jr.

INTRODUCTION
6, Mickey Pfleger; 8, Mike Powell/Allsport; 9, Hy Peskin; 10, George Tiedemann; 11, Fred Vuich.

CLASSIC PERFORMANCES
12-13, Jerry Cooke; 14, Heinz Kluetmeier; 14-15, Bettmann/CORBIS; 15, Neil Leifer; 17, NFL Photos; 18, NFL Photos; 21, Holly Stein/Allsport; 23, Steve Cadrain; 25, Scott Halleran/Allsport; 27, Milwaukee Journal; 29, Rich Clarkson; 30, Mike Powell/Allsport; 32, Manny Millan; 34, Mark Kauffman; 36, Manchete; 39, Bettmann/CORBIS; 41, Hy Peskin; 43, Neil Leifer; 44, Bill Frakes; 47, AP; 49, Oxford Daily Mail; 50, Eric Schweikardt; 53, James Drake; 54, AP; 55, AP; 57, Neil Leifer; 58-59, Neil Leifer; 60, top, Neil Leifer; bottom, Jerry Cooke; 62, Wide World Photos/AP; 65, Tony Duffy/Allsport.

SPECTACULAR SEASONS
66-67, Damian Strohmeyer; 68, Heinz Kluetmeier; 68-69, Walter Iooss Jr.; 69, Laurence Griffiths/Allsport; 70-71, Ben Radford/Allsport; 73, Walter Iooss Jr.; 74, Damian Strohmeyer; 77, AP; 78, V. J. Lovero; 81, Walter Iooss Jr.; 83, Underwood & Underwood/Corbis; 85, Rich Clarkson; 86-87, Walter Iooss Jr.; 88, top, Neil Leifer; bottom, Neil Leifer; 89, Sheedy & Long; 90, Baseball Hall of Fame Library; 92, Bettmann/CORBIS; inset, Transcendental Graphics; 92-93, Bettmann/CORBIS.

LEGENDARY STREAKS
94-95, Bettmann/CORBIS; 96, Walter Iooss Jr.; 96-97, Walter Iooss Jr; 97, John Biever; 99, Olivier Labalette/Tempsport/Newsport; 101, Heinz Kluetmeier; 103, John G. Zimmerman; 105, Sheedy & Long; 107, Walter Iooss Jr.; 108, John Biever; 111, Hy Peskin; 113, Wide World Photos/AP; 114, Hy Peskin; 117, Jerry Wachter; 119, Trevor Jones; 120, Sheedy & Long; 122, Rich Clarkson; 122-123, Sheedy & Long; 124, John Biever; 126, Robert Beck; 126-127, Bob Martin; 129, Transcendental Graphics; 130-131, Bettmann/CORBIS; 132-133, Acme Newspictures Inc./Sports Illustrated Picture Collection; 133, AP.

A LIFETIME OF EXCELLENCE
94-95, Bettmann/CORBIS; 96, Walter Iooss Jr.; 96-97, Walter Iooss Jr; 134-135, Peter Read Miller; 136, David E. Klutho; 136-137, John Iacono; 137, Tom Rampy; 138, Graphic Artists/Hockey Hall of Fame; 140, Gerry Cranham; 143, Hy Peskin; 145, Rich Clarkson; 147, Daily News; 148, Peter Read Miller; 151, John G. Zimmerman; 152, George Tiedemann; 154-155, Tom Rampy; 155, Wayne Wilson/Leviton-Atlanta; 156, Baseball Hall of Fame Library; 159, Peter Read Miller; 160, James Drake; 162, James Drake; 163, Heinz Kluetmeier; 164, Paul J. Bereswill; 166, David E. Klutho; 166-167, Robert Beck.

HONORABLE MENTION
168, CORBIS; 169, Peter Read Miller; 170, George Tiedemann/GT images; 171, Shaun Best/Reuters/Timepix.

INDEX